THE BABY BOOMERS SURVIVAL HANDBOOK FOR THE 21ST CENTURY

Essential Strategies for Mental, Physical,
Financial, Social, and Spiritual Success

By
Samuel J. Tucker, Ph.D.

The information and procedures contained in this book are based upon research. They are not intended as a substitute for consulting with your physician or other health care provider. The publisher and author are not responsible for any adverse effects or consequences resulting from the use of any of the suggestions, preparations, or procedures discussed in this book. All matters pertaining to your physical health should be supervised by a health care professional.

Library of Congress Catalog Card Number
98-093756
ISBN 09666194-0-4

Dedication

This book is dedicated to Arlene, my wife, my best critic, my best friend, and to our four children and their spouses: Samuel, Jr., Sabrina and Michael Hall, Sharon and Mohammed Belhamel, Sterling and Danuelle Tucker; my three grandchildren, Michael Hall, Jr., Marcus Hall, Sterling Tucker, Jr., and to all of the Baby Boomers.

Contents

Preface

The great Dr. Albert Einstein was asked the question, "Why are we here?" Here is a man who understood more about the laws governing the universe than any person in history. Dr. Einstein believed that there is meaning in the universe and that such a magnificent and colossal order of the universe could not have been an accident. He said, "The more I study physics, the more I am drawn toward metaphysics." Dr. Einstein answered the question, "Why are we here?" by stating that we are here for the sake of others.

In a quest to serve others, I have written this book to serve the Baby Boomers of the twenty-first century. The book is not intended to be a survey of research literature. It is a book designed to help Baby Boomers with the skills that I feel will be needed to successfully survive during the twenty-first century. I have tried to provide the readers with certain tools so that they may evaluate their present life for themselves. If you find something you don't like about yourself or your present status, you will learn the procedures for modification. It has been said that we are the product of two gods—the one that gave us the gift of life and two, our own behavior to make our life a gift to God.

The traditional self-help books have been written to consider one or two areas of a person's life. However, people do not compartmentalize their day-to-day living. You do not act as an economic being one day, a political being the next, a religious being the next, and so on. Rather, you act as a whole being. Therefore, this book is a comprehensive self-help approach to the quest of successful living in the twenty-first century.

This book is a compilation of research and effective self-help strategies pertaining to all significant areas of a person's life. Successful achievement is not the result of implementing a single technique or approach. I hope you will find as much value in these research findings and strategies for success as many of my students and patients have over the years. I wish to remind you that knowledge makes all things possible. If you open your mind, you will open your future to unlimited possibilities. I believe as Napoleon Hill said, "You have absolute control over but one thing—and that is your thoughts. If you fail to control your own mind, you may be sure you will control nothing else."

Samuel J. Tucker, Ph.D.

Acknowledgments

I am indebted to many people, schools, and organizations who assisted me in various ways during the time I was collecting data and writing this book. They include the alumni of the various schools I attended: Parker High School, Morehouse College, Clark Atlanta University, Columbia University, Harvard University; colleges where I served as a faculty member: The University of Florida and Alabama State University; colleges where I served as president: Edward Waters College and Langston University.

Introduction

Everyone knows and loves Peter Pan, that adventurous kid who never wanted to grow up. Well, many members of the Baby Boom generation[1] are like that, thinking that they will never give up their youth or never grow old. Numerous articles have been written emphasizing how the Baby Boomers will transform our notions of aging and what it means to be middle-aged in America.

Employment, health care, housing, education, and leisure-time activities are only a few of the many areas that will be affected as the Boomers approach their mid-life mark and beyond. For example, Baby Boomers are expected to work longer and to have second or even third careers, either part-time or full-time. They also will travel more and will spend more on health products and personal fitness as well as on entertainment and other recreational activities.

The first Boomers are already in their early fifties, and during the next decade about 10,000 additional Americans will turn fifty *every day.*

As more and more Boomers reach the big "5-0" in their personal lifeline, reality slowly begins to sink in. Unlike their parents and grandparents, many Boomers have not planned adequately for the future and cannot expect to live as well in retirement. Although Boomers as a group will inherit about $1 trillion during the next ten years as their parents pass away, a good portion of which they will

---

[1]"Baby Boomers" are the 76 million Americans born between 1946 and 1964. *Fortune* magazine was the first to coin and use this term.

Baby Boomers Aged Fifty and Older

Year	Number of Boomers
1996	2.9 million
2000	17.2 million
2005	36.3 million
2010	57.1 million
2015	76 million

probably invest, only a relatively few can expect a "windfall" from a parent. The reality is that when many Boomers reach their sixties and seventies, not only will they have to worry about supporting themselves, but they may have to provide at least partial financial support for one or both parents who are in their eighties or nineties.

It's not just financial planning that is important. As more and more Boomers reach the age of fifty, they must begin to develop a system that will help them organize every aspect of their lives in preparation for their "Golden Years." Some of the many questions that maturing Baby Boomers must confront as they approach middle age include:

- Do I want to spend the rest of my working life in my present career?
- What would a career change mean at this point in my life, and how would it affect the lives of my spouse and children?
- How do I acquire financial security for myself and my family?
- At what age would I like to retire, and how will I provide for my retirement?
- What changes can I begin to make now to ensure better physical and psychological health for the rest of my life?

This book has been written to help Boomers create the ideal life and lifestyle they have always dreamed about but have yet to attain. It is a practical survival guide targeted to those individuals who want to learn how to exert more control over the many areas of their lives that can be changed before it is too late. You will learn how to analyze your aspirations and goals, how to mount your individual campaign for achievement, and how to measure that achievement on a regular basis. Techniques designed to improve self-esteem, as well as methods to improve the quality of social relationships, are discussed. The latest theories regarding diet, exercise, and lifestyle changes are explored to help you maximize your physical and mental health. Meditation and other methods for enhancing your emotional well-being and your spirituality are presented. Ways to acquire financial security and freedom from debt through financial consultations and investments are provided.

During ancient time, knowledge was shared only in secret societies and was not taught to the masses. Today, we live in the information age where people residing in even the most remote areas of the world have access to such information outlets as the fax machine, CNN, and the Internet. If we are going to be successful, it will depend on our knowledge and, to a large extent, our technical skills, rather than on our physical strength as during the time of our forefathers.

Roadmaps exist for survival in the twenty-first century. Scientists have been working for many years in laboratories, hospitals, senior-citizen homes, and many other facilities studying problems of human behavior. Their findings have been published in professional journals, abstracts, books, and scholarly papers. This handbook will simplify some of these abstract human research studies, setting forth the valuable conclusions and selecting the best techniques that can be used to help the average person be more successful in the twenty-first century. This book is about *you*—how you live now and how you dream about living in the future. If you want to improve the quality of your life and want to enjoy growing older with more style and grace, this book is for you.

Chapter 1

Your Personal Profile—Getting Reacquainted with Yourself

"Knowing who you are and what you are will give you the self-confidence to begin to take control of your life."

Before delving into the practical details of planning your future, we would like you to perform a few easy (and fun) exercises designed to help you discover (or rediscover) your special interests and dreams and to assist you in learning more about the kind of person you are.

A roadmap is not of much use unless you know where you are located. Before you can redirect your energies and become focused, it is necessary to undergo an honest self-appraisal of where you are now. How many years has it been since you've taken inventory of your personal life? To begin, ask yourself the following questions:

- What are my likes and dislikes?
- How do I prefer to spend my leisure time?
- What subject areas would I like to study and learn more about?
- What career or job would I love to have if I could choose anything in the world, even if I didn't get paid for doing it?

Please don't jump to the conclusion that "filling in the blanks" in these exercises is too simplistic an approach. After all, you may be a very successful person with an unusually clear and comprehensive understanding about your own psychological makeup and motivations. Just keep in mind, however, that no individual's dreams, fantasies, or personality remain static. You may be surprised to learn that more than a few of your likes and dislikes—as well as your dreams and ambitions—have changed substantially over the years

1

without your being consciously aware of it. By performing these few exercises, you just might learn something new about yourself!

Also, be sure to write down all your answers to the various questions. An organized and written list of your interests, dreams, objectives, and goals will help clarify your thinking and will make the task of achieving them much easier.

EXERCISE 1.1—Your Pleasure Points

To begin, write down the six activities or interests that give you the greatest pleasure, the things you love to do the most, without regard to how well you do them. Feel free to list any activities for which you have been complimented in the past, but only if these are things you really enjoy. For example, don't list "cooking" or "entertaining friends," even though everyone raves about your meals and your parties, unless this is something you personally enjoy very much.

If you love spending time with your family, shopping at the mall, reading, gardening, talking on the phone with friends, exercising, camping/hiking/backpacking, singing in your church choir, doing volunteer work, etc., then write it down. You may be a person with scores of different interests and activities, and it may be difficult for you to select only a few from among them all, but try to whittle your list down to the six activities you enjoy the most at this particular period in your life.

1.

2.

3.

4.

5.

6.

After you have competed the list, spend some time analyzing it, thinking about *why* you enjoy doing the things you selected. Do you see any patterns beginning to emerge? For example, did you include activities that primarily involve your home and family or your children's school or your church? Do you enjoy activities that are mentally stimulating or ones that are more physical in nature? Perhaps you will discover that the things that give you the greatest pleasure are activities you perform mostly alone, or perhaps the majority of your interests involve other people.

EXERCISE 1.2—Your Dream Job or Career

If you could have any career or job in the world, even if you didn't have the necessary skills and training for it, what would you most like to do with the rest of your life? Think carefully about this, and write your top three choices in the spaces provided here.

1.

2.

3.

Next, let's vary the question a little. If you could immediately change jobs or careers, what would you most like to do that you are presently qualified for or soon could be? Try to mesh your present age, personality, lifestyle, education, and so forth with your dream job or career. For example, in this exercise don't say that you would like to be a world-class athlete if you are middle-aged and have led a sedentary life for the past two or three decades. Likewise, don't say you would like to be a college professor, a doctor, or a lawyer if your formal education is limited and you know for sure that you cannot (or would not) be able to spend the many years necessary studying to be a professor, doctor, or lawyer.

List your top three choices.

1.

2.

3.

EXERCISE 1.3—Subjects or Areas about Which You Want to Learn More

Next, make a list of at least six subjects or specialty training areas that you would like to know more about. If you had all the time in the world, which courses or subjects would you most like to study, what training would you like to receive?

Do you want to learn more about computers? Would you like to develop the skills to someday build your own home or to become a landscape designer? Have you ever dreamed of studying to become a travel agent or a real estate agent? Would you like to learn what is involved in opening a restaurant or a retail store or starting some other business of your own? Have you ever wanted to learn to play a musical instrument? Maybe you are academically inclined and have always wanted to study art, psychology, or theology, or perhaps you've thought about how interesting it would be if you could become fluent in a foreign language. Have you ever dreamed of learning how to write sellable articles or books? Perhaps you're one of the millions of people fascinated at the possibility of tracing your family roots and you'd like to learn how to do research in this area.

Although the possibilities in this exercise are endless, don't go wild here. Think about it carefully—if you had the necessary time and the money, what six subject areas would you like to study most?

1.

2.

3.

4.

5.

6.

EXERCISE 1.4—Your Personal Strengths

In this exercise we want you to list six personal strengths and attributes—not necessarily skills but rather personality traits and qualities—that make you unique and that have brought you compliments and praise in the past.

Are you a kind and empathetic person? Are you patient and adaptable? Do you forgive and forget easily? Are you especially friendly or a good listener? Do you think positively? Are you usually optimistic? Do you hold up well under stress? Do you persevere? Are you resourceful?

These personal strengths are but a few examples of positive traits that may or may not apply to you. Put your thinking cap on and try to determine the six key positive strengths that describe you best. Don't hesitate to brag about yourself!

1.

2.

3.

4.

5.

6.

EXERCISE 1.5—Your Personal Weaknesses

Just as we all have our own personal strengths, we also have our weaknesses. It is important that you spend some time thinking about and writing down what you consider to be your most obvious weaknesses. Try to be as honest with yourself as possible. This exercise is designed to help you to get to know yourself better, and your list is confidential—you don't have to show it to anyone else.

Are you short-tempered and irritable? Are you vain or jealous? Are you overcritical or intolerant? Do you engage in malicious gossip? Are you rude, especially with strangers who might get in your way? Do you interrupt others when they are making a point? Do you procrastinate? Are you always late for appointments? Do you "waste" time? Do you worry too much about trivial matters?

List your six most obvious personal weaknesses.

1.

2.

3.

4.

5.

6.

If you have performed each of the exercises with as much care and candor as possible, you have surely discovered a few things about yourself. You have determined what you enjoy doing the most, you have indicated what your three dream jobs or career choices would be and the subject areas you would like to learn more about, you have analyzed and listed your individual strengths and weaknesses, and you have identified your most important goals and objectives.

Over the next several days and weeks, re-examine your responses in each of the exercises and think about them as often as you can. During this period of contemplation, you may realize that you have overlooked some important items. Perhaps you failed to list something you enjoy doing very much, or you may have inadvertently omitted one or more personal characteristics (positive or negative) that you now deem important. Feel free to make alterations to your lists as you go along.

Also, give some thought to the three subjects or specialty training areas that you would like to learn more about and try to determine the best way for you to actually begin to study one or all of these subjects. Review your goals and make your own personal list of exactly what you will have to do to reach each and every one of them within the timeline you have selected.

The purpose of this chapter is to get you to embark on the path of self-discovery or rediscovery because, as we stated at the beginning of the chapter, knowing who you are and what you are will give you the self-confidence to begin to take control of your life.

Chapter 2

Taking Control

"All that you ever do or aspire to do will be predicated on two basic concepts—self-esteem and self-control. How you feel about yourself and how much control you believe you have will ultimately determine how well you perform in every area of your life."

We have no control over the circumstances of our birth—where we are born and when, who our parents are, the genes we inherit (good or bad), our socioeconomic background, our race, the color of our skin, or our physical appearance. In general, we also have no control over when and how we are going to die. However, after we reach a certain age and a certain degree of maturity, we do have an enormous amount of control over the sort of life we live in the relatively short interval between adulthood and death.

Almost everyone daydreams at times about the radical changes and improvements they would make in their lives if they suddenly won a lot of money from the lottery or from another source. They might envision buying a larger and nicer home or car, sending their children to a first-rate private college, or taking long, leisurely trips around the world. Some people dream about the successful career they hope to have in their chosen profession as soon as they get their graduate degree. Others spend literally years fantasizing about one day quitting their job and finally telling their boss or supervisor what they really think of him or her before going off to start their own business or trade.

These daydreams and fantasies of a different—and much better—life for ourselves and for our families are often what keeps us going, month in and month out, year in and year out. If we didn't have these dreams, if we didn't believe deep in our hearts that one day—somehow, someway—our lives were going to get better, then there would be little reason to keep trying.

Far too many people lose their dreams along the way and become unable to cope with the stresses and vagaries of life and of approaching middle age. They may get in a rut, experience extreme burn-out, or just lose their zest for living. It is a well-known fact that a variety of physical and emotional problems result when a person loses his or her capacity to cope with the stresses of everyday life, at home, on the job, or socially. Many of the diseases and ailments of the body that plague people in middle age—such as high blood pressure, asthma, allergies, colitis, headaches, backaches, or sexual dysfunctions—often have an emotional component as their cause. This intensity of emotional distress is reflected in the statistics. In contrast to their elders, members of the Baby Boomer generation have higher rates of psychiatric illness and are much more likely to seek mental health services. Statistics also reveal that most suicides occur after the age of forty.

Often the mere process of self-evaluation and self-reflection will cause many individuals to experience anxiety, depression, and emotional turmoil. Some of this comes from the realization that an interminable future, where anything and everything is possible, no longer exists. Coming to terms with the realities of life and of the future can be a very wrenching experience—emotionally and intellectually.

It doesn't have to be this way. What many people fail to realize is that even without suddenly becoming rich, even without someday finding that dream job or career, they already possess the power to change many important aspects of their everyday lives and to forge ahead toward a brighter and happier future.

What is required is a will and determination to change and a sensible and realistic plan to effect that change.

It is important to understand that the significant changes in life usually occur as a result of a series of small, incremental changes, both in your attitude and in your behavior. In order to bring your dreams to fruition and change your external world—to get a better job or develop new career possibilities, to make more money, to enjoy better physical and psychological health, and to experience a happier family life and a richer social life—you must change on the inside as well as on the outside. You must develop more self-confidence and more self-esteem, because the way you view yourself will affect your performance in every area of your life.

Developing a Healthy Self-Esteem[1]

Your self-image or self-esteem affects virtually every aspect of your existence—the way you function at work and at home, the way you operate as a spouse or a parent, how you behave in love and in sex, and how you relate to your friends and to the world at large. A healthy self-image is not something we are born with. It is learned and developed in the early years of our lives as we internalize the views, feelings, and evaluations of significant others around us. Parents and other family members, teachers, playmates, and peers all strongly influence a young person's self-concept and self-esteem. Even something as seemingly innocent as a nickname given to a child can become a vital part of that child's view of himself or herself—a view that may persist over a lifetime. Thus, a teenager who is looked upon as intelligent or dumb, as attractive or homely, as obnoxious or friendly, begins to see himself or herself in the roles ascribed by others and begins to behave accordingly.

A number of articles and books have been written about the deleterious effects that poverty, discrimination, and lack of opportunity have on the self-image of disadvantaged members of minority groups. It has been shown, for example, that some inner-city children perform poorly academically in accordance with the self-image that has been given them most of their lives by their parents and teachers.

Social psychologists have shown us that people tend to perform as they are expected to perform. For example, there is a well-known experiment conducted by a primary school teacher with her young pupils. She told her class that recent scientific reports have verified that children with blue eyes have greater natural abilities than children with brown eyes. After a few weeks of closely observing her class, this teacher noted that the achievement level of the children

---

[1]In this chapter and throughout this book, we will use the terms "self-image," "self-concept," and "self-esteem" interchangeably. In our use of the terms, they all mean virtually the same thing—how much you like yourself, how you feel about yourself.

with brown eyes fell measurably, while the performance of the children with blue eyes improved significantly.

She then made another announcement to her class, that she had made a mistake, that the scientific reports actually showed that the students with blue eyes were "weaker" academically and the children with brown eyes were actually the "stronger" (i.e., better) students.

Guess what happened next! Believe it or not, the achievement and performance level of the students in the brown eyes group went up measurably, and that of the blue eyes group went down. These results proved that those students who are regarded as brighter than their classmates actually performed much better.

Self-image determines the kind of person you are and influences your success or failure when you start trying to change your behavior and your lifestyle. A positive self-image will enhance your confidence in your own judgment and abilities and will increase the likelihood that you will feel capable of dealing with adversity. The person who can attribute at least part of the failures and deficiencies he encounters to the external world rather than to his own personal limitations is able to maintain a higher view of his own self-worth and will achieve more in life.

You can develop more self-esteem and self-confidence by understanding that you are unique with special talents and skills. Although talent is a natural, inborn inclination for doing something well, there are countless abilities and skills that can be acquired through learning and practice. You have had and will continue to have experiences unlike those of anyone else in the world. Granted, there are areas where others will excel more than you, just as there are areas where you can achieve more than others. You can't do everything better than everyone else, and it is foolish to expect to achieve perfection in all areas. However, you can discover where your talents lie, and you can begin to harness and utilize *your* unique talents and skills.

EXERCISE 2.1—Evaluating Your Self-Regard and Self-Esteem

To get an assessment of your own self-esteem, ask yourself the questions in the following exercise:

• Do I view myself as a winner or a loser?
• Do I see myself as strong and capable or weak and inefficient?

- When I take on a project or task, and the going gets rough, do I have the confidence and courage to persevere or do I say, "I'll never be able to do that" and just give up in frustration?
- Have I made a serious effort to know myself?

Changing Your Attitudes

How important are attitudes? Social psychologists believe your attitudes can strongly influence your daily life and destiny. William James, the famous nineteenth-century psychologist said, ". . . a man can change his life by changing his attitude toward himself and his work." In fact, research shows that people who believe they have some control over their lives are most likely to succeed. The losers in life believe luck controls their destiny, and they go through life lamenting their bad luck. Instead of taking concrete steps to change their lives, they muddle on, hoping that their luck will eventually change for the better.

Sometimes people develop self-defeating attitudes because of life's disappointments. You may once have had a positive outlook and engaged in positive actions but still failed in a certain area. Therefore, you have subsequently adopted the comfortable stance of avoiding disappointment by expecting the worst and hoping for the best. In time, you developed habitual patterns of acting and reacting that reflect your attitudes. This can occur consciously or unconsciously. These negative behaviors or habits might alleviate perceived pain, but they prohibit potential growth.

The term "self-fulfilling prophecy" came about because attitude is so compelling it can influence your behavior. This term suggests that if you believe something bad is going to happen, more than likely you'll bring about the thing you fear through your actions. Take, for example, an insecure husband or wife who believes their spouse is going to leave them. This person can bring about this prophecy through certain actions (i.e., accusations, jealousy, threats, etc.). Similarly, if you feel you cannot succeed in certain areas, you may avoid taking the chances necessary for your success. Your negative thinking can thus lead to failure.

Samuel Johnson, who lived in the eighteenth century, is quoted as saying, "The chains of habit are too weak to be felt until they are too strong to be broken." Similarly, our self-defeating thoughts and attitudes can chain us to mediocrity unless we exercise our power of choice to make changes.

An important factor in whether or not we make successful changes is optimism—thinking positively. We are all familiar with the story of the glass with a certain amount of liquid in it. The optimist says the glass is half full; the pessimist says it is half empty. Despite the objective reality that a 16-ounce glass may contain only 8 ounces of liquid, the optimist and the pessimist reflect vast differences in attitude.

There are countless books and self-help tapes that emphasize the power of an optimistic attitude. There is a good reason for the proliferation of these materials—an optimistic outlook on life can influence all areas of your self-development.

How do you break free from self-defeating attitudes to adopt a positive outlook on life? Before you can take control of your own destiny, you must have the courage to recognize the negative attitudes that have been holding you back.

Ask yourself the questions listed in the following exercise and answer them as candidly as possible.

EXERCISE 2.2—Evaluating Your Attitude

- Are my attitudes negative and self-defeating?
- Do my attitudes prevent me from pursuing my dreams?
- Do my attitudes inhibit me from pursuing the relationships I desire?
- In ambiguous situations, do I tend to assume the worst?
- Do I feel that my life is controlled by destiny, and no matter what I do the outcome will be the same?
- Do I avoid situations or tasks in which I think I might fail?
- Is my glass half empty?

In the following chart, please write down at least six self-defeating and negative attitudes in the left column, and for each one list a positive counter-attitude in the right column. First, write down those attitudes that apply to you personally, then if you have any space left, you can include the negative attitudes of some of your friends or family members.

Self-Defeating Attitudes	Positive Counter-Attitudes
Example: I don't have the skills to succeed in the career or job I want most.	*Example: I can study and train myself to become qualified for my dream job.*
1.	1.
2.	2.
3.	3.
4.	4.
5.	5.
6.	6.

EXERCISE 2.3—Evaluating Your Behavior

Just as you did, in the previous section, please answer the following questions about your behavior:

- If I had only one year to live, what are some of the things that I would like to accomplish?
- What are my goals for the next twelve months?
- What goals do I have for my mental, physical, financial, social, and spiritual development?

In the left column of the following chart, please write down six self-defeating and negative behaviors that apply to you personally or to your friends and family. In the right column of the chart, indicate the most appropriate positive or counter-behavior.

Self-Defeating Behaviors	Positive Counter-Behaviors
1.	1.
2.	2.
3.	3.
4.	4.
5.	5.
6.	6.

Changing Yourself

The objective of taking inventory of your negative and self-defeating attitudes and behaviors is to assess them so that they will no longer hold you back from success. Each time you find yourself confronted with a situation that triggers a negative attitude or behavior, make a conscious decision to act with a positive one instead. The process won't be easy, but as you begin to think and act more positively, you will begin to build a solid foundation. No matter how negative and defeating your attitudes or behaviors may be, when you take action, step by step, no obstacle is insurmountable.

It is important that you undertake this project one step at a time. If you had a house that needed painting, for example, looking at the whole task could be intimidating, but if you look at the house room by room, you realize you have the power and confidence to complete the task. The same is true for replacing the negative attitudes and behaviors that hold you back from success. An honest assessment may lead you to identify a number of areas for improvement. Tackling them one at a time will build confidence in your ability to change and improve. Like painting a house, this process is not one huge, difficult job. It is a series of small tasks that can be accomplished.

As you master the art of replacing old self-defeating attitudes and behaviors with positive ones, you will begin to notice that in new situations, positive attitudes and behaviors will become more frequent and habit-forming.

Chapter 3

The Road to Success—Getting Started

Don't make the mistake of assuming that achievement and success come only by some quirk of fate, chance, or luck. Success is achieved by analyzing a problem or endeavor, breaking it down into small units or sub-units, and then taking the practical, concrete steps necessary to reach your desired goals.

There are several key areas that need to be developed and maintained in order for a person to achieve a successful life and a well-balanced lifestyle. Neglect of any one of these over an extended period of time will put that person at grave risk and peril. These important areas are:

- Personal
- Physical
- Mental/Intellectual
- Social
- Emotional/Spiritual
- Financial

Let's take a brief look at a few specific examples.

To live well and to function at our fullest capacity, both physical and psychological health is a must. Without a healthy body and an optimistic and positive mental attitude, it matters little how much financial or career success we achieve. In all the surveys ever conducted on whether it is more important to have good health or great wealth, health was chosen over wealth by a landslide.

Similarly, no one would dispute the importance of finding time in our busy lives for socialization, recreation, or "fun." It is an ironic fact, however, that many people become so frantic and so fanatical about developing their careers or businesses that not only do they have little or no time to relax and have fun, but they actually lose their capacity to do so.

Financial security is essential, but driving oneself day and night to earn more and more money only to topple over suddenly with a heart attack or another serious illness is definitely not the way to do it. This is a classic example of overemphasizing one particular area of life while neglecting some of the other areas.

How do you begin to mesh and balance all these key areas and live a well-rounded and truly successful life?

- First, try to determine exactly what you wish to achieve in each area. Think about your goals and objectives, write them down, and discuss them with family members and friends whose opinions you trust.
- Second, make a detailed evaluation of the requirements needed to reach your goals. Write down both short-term and long-term strategies needed to implement them. Set up a schedule of deadlines.
- Third, don't procrastinate; don't put off getting started. It is necessary to set specific dates—timelines—to implement pertinent procedures to surmount barriers. Determine your initiation date and completion date.
- Fourth, carefully identify and define the barriers that stand between you and your goal.
- Fifth, find rational solutions for each problem; analyze the situation and create methods for crossing each hurdle; there is almost no problem that cannot be overcome in time.
- Sixth, make use of affirmations and meditation.

Throughout this book we will emphasize repeatedly the importance of making desired changes in your life and lifestyle through a series of small steps, rather than waiting to begin a major overhaul of your life—someday. The "someday" may never come, and you may find yourself a decade or two older without being any closer to your dreams and goals than you are today.

One example—if you decide the way to better physical health is through exercise, start your new regimen immediately by walking more or climbing stairs instead of riding the elevator. Don't wait until next week or next month or next year to begin the "perfect" and more time-consuming exercise program. Just getting started is what's important now.

Making Resolutions for Change

At the beginning of each new year most of us make resolutions that we are determined to stick with for at least a few months. How many people do you know who start a new diet every year in early January? How many swear that this is the year they will stop smoking, start exercising more, or that they will get out of debt before the next new year rolls around? We all know these people. We ourselves are these people. Inevitably, however, year in and year out, we seldom make it beyond mid-January with many of our resolutions, and by the end of January we have usually just given up and have fallen back into our old routines and habits.

There's nothing wrong with making resolutions each year on January 1. But if we make them and break them, why do we need to wait an entire year before getting started again? Why can't we make new resolutions (or at least reaffirm our old ones) at the beginning of each and every month?

It is a proven fact that the person who makes smaller, more manageable resolutions twelve times a year, instead of just once on January 1, is the person who will ultimately achieve the greatest success in every aspect of his or her life. For example, if you want to lose weight, instead of resolving to lose 40 pounds during the next six months, why not resolve to lose seven pounds in January, another seven pounds in February, and so on until you reach your ultimate goal?

Your actual weight loss per month may not be any different than when you resolved to lose a larger amount over a longer period of time, but as you see yourself achieving your goal each and every month, your mental attitude will change and your self-confidence and self-esteem will get a tremendous boost.

We are all familiar with the old saying that "Success breeds success." The same is true of a commitment to change—make a few small changes to begin with (even if you have to struggle to do so) and soon they will snowball. Part of the new behavior has to do with the fact that small changes and improvements eventually add up to larger and more substantial changes. Much of the achievement involves the simple fact that if you stick to a plan or commitment long enough, your self-confidence will grow as well, thus making it easier for you to take whatever risks are necessary to achieve your goals in the future.

Don't make the mistake of assuming that achievement and success come only by some quirk of fate, chance, or luck. Success is achieved by analyzing a problem or endeavor, breaking it down into small units or sub-units, and then taking the practical, concrete steps necessary to reach your desired goals.

How do you get started? You make up your mind that you will achieve a certain goal, and then you find the time and financial resources needed to reach it. When people talk about wanting to change some aspect of their life, inevitably they lament the fact that they don't have the time or money to begin to propel themselves on the road to success. This is negative thinking at its worst, as a brief analysis of these two complaints will prove.

Time Management—An Overview

Most people have not given it much thought, so they do not realize that there are 168 hours in a week and that the average person has at least 60 hours a week of "free time" when they aren't sleeping, working or eating. *This totals about 250 hours of free time per month.* Of course, some of this free time will be spent with family or friends or engaging in enjoyable activities and hobbies. Unfortunately, however, not all free time is utilized time; a large portion of it is "wasted time."

Consider the number of hours you spend each week talking to friends on the phone about trivialities or the hours spent slouched in front of the TV watching a boring re-run or a lengthy sports event. And do you really need to surf the Internet and visit your favorite chat rooms *every* night? Why not unplug your phone for an hour or two each evening, or turn the TV and the computer off a few evenings a week, and get down to the business of planning your future?

What about the hours you spend commuting to and from work each week? Could you start doing something worthwhile with this time? If you commute by automobile, why not listen to audio books or lectures instead of talking on your cell phone and fussing and fuming at every driver who pulls in front of you or changes lanes without signaling. If you use public transportation, why not read or study instead of staring out the window or glaring at your fellow passengers?

These are just a few examples of how people can waste lots of time every week without giving it too much thought. Although the examples mentioned are not negative activities by themselves, it is the amount of time spent on them on a regular basis that brings in the element of negativity.

If you are serious about wanting to learn a new subject, develop a new skill, or find the time to plan your future, why not resolve to set aside a certain amount of your "free time" each week or month? You won't have to give up any of the leisure-time activities that you enjoy most, but if you spend only 50 hours per month on something new and worthwhile, within a few short months you will surely have begun to master it. Keep in mind that there are 720 hours in a 30-day month; thus, even our arbitrary number of 50 hours is only a small fraction of your total monthly time.

One important caveat—it would be ideal if you could set aside a certain amount of time every day to pursue your dreams and goals, but this is probably not practical or realistic because of the setbacks that will inevitably occur on a regular basis. You may have to work late several days in a row, someone in your family may become ill and require your attention, friends may come to visit, or in spite of your best efforts you may get distracted in other ways. A viable alternative approach, therefore, might be to spend one or two evenings a week or perhaps a large portion of the day on Saturday or Sunday in pursuit of your goals.

The old cliché, "Where there's a will, there's a way," is appropriate here. If you make up your mind that you are going to do something, then you *will* find the necessary time to do it.

Time Management—The $25,000 Idea

Years ago, the president of a large industrial corporation was approached by an aggressive efficiency expert who hoped to make the company a client of his firm. The corporation president told the efficiency expert that his company already had plenty of management techniques and what he needed was a system to accomplish more. The efficiency expert handed the president a piece of paper and a pen. He asked him to write down, in order of importance, the five most pressing things he had to do the next day. He was then instructed to think about each item he had listed and to estimate how long it would take him to complete each task.

The president was further instructed to tackle the first item with a vengeance when he arrived at his desk in the morning and to work at it until it was completed before going on to the next task, and so on down the list until every item on the list had been handled.

The corporation president tried this technique for a period of time and later sent the efficiency expert a check for $25,000 for the idea.

The embodiment of this technique is called the "priority points" method. It can change the course of your daily working life and of your associates' daily working life.

This simple method really works! Why? Because you can do only one major thing at a time. Worrying about the other jobs doesn't help. Trying to handle all of them at once means that you probably won't finish *any* of them correctly. Nothing is more frustrating than doing yesterday's work today.

Money Management—An Overview

In addition to wasting time, people also waste money—a lot of money. It has been estimated that the average person "squanders" at least one or two dollars of every ten dollars they earn on nonessential items and incidentals.

To illustrate this point, let's say that a person's weekly gross earnings are in the neighborhood of $800 to $850 and that the net earnings are about $600 per week. If this person "wastes" 10 percent of the net income each week, that totals over $3,000 by the end of a year. In only five short years, this "squandered" money would amount to more than $15,000! This is money that has just gone down the drain, so to speak, with nothing tangible or worthwhile to show for it. It is gone forever.

Your rejoinder may be that you don't want to be a miser, that you enjoy your "little treats." Do you have to spend so much on incidentals and nonessentials? Why not attempt to save at least a portion of it? We are not going to tell you how you should spend your "pin money"; we merely want to point out to you in a compelling way that a few dollars saved or invested (even as small an amount as $50 or $60 per week) can add up to a substantial sum over a period of time.

These illustrations are presented in order to get you to begin to think seriously about your own situation regarding time and money. We hope that you will begin to understand how it is possible to better utilize your time and save more money, if you really put your mind to it. More on investing will be discussed in the chapter on financial action strategies.

Setting Goals

People who use a systematic, proven method of goal setting and goal attainment accomplish goals at a higher rate than the average person. You need to set goals that are multidimensional. You need to set goals for every part of your life. Like a balanced wheel that goes around smoothly in every respect, you need goals for your mental and physical health, for your career, for your finances, for your relationships, for your social development, and for your spiritual growth. Nothing happens by accident. Everything happens for a reason. You are the primary creative force in your own life; you are the main cause. Things will happen in your life because you make them happen, not because you sit around and wait for them to happen.

Step 1. Decide exactly what you want. The most important single quality of goal-setting and of success is clarity. Conclude in finite terms what you want in each area of your life. For example, set specific and concrete numbers about how much extra money you want to earn in a specific period of time or specify exactly what level of health and fitness you desire. Stay away from generalized or fuzzy goals such as "I want to earn more money," or "I want to enjoy better health."

It is imperative to have a goal or objective that deeply motivates you. To get the best out of yourself, recognize this and remember that *it is from deep within you that your strongest mission comes.* You need a personal mission—a meaningful project that propels you to invest yourself in accomplishing because it is the goal you really care about achieving.

Step 2. Write down your goals. Most people think about written goals and plan to write them down, someday, but only a small percentage of adults actually write down their goals. The majority just never get around to it and will spend more time making a list of groceries before they go shopping or planning a vacation than they do in planning their lives. Success begins with a pad of paper, a pen, and a few minutes of your time.

One of the most important keys to success is to think on paper. If you cannot write your goal down clearly and specifically on a piece of paper, then it means that you are not really clear about the goal yourself and perhaps you do not really want it.

Step 3. Set a deadline. Don't be intimidated by large goals—break them down by setting a series of smaller, more short-term deadlines. Your subconscious mind reacts to a deadline as a "forcing system" and begins to move you rapidly towards your goals.

Step 4. Make a list of everything you can imagine that will help you achieve your goal. You will believe strongly and become more motivated if your list is quite comprehensive.

Step 5. Take your list and organize it into a plan. A plan is a list organized by priority and importance. You decide what you will accomplish first and what you will do later—in other words, what is more important and what is less important. You are the only person who can decide the single thing that is more important than anything else and what you can do immediately to begin moving towards your goal.

Step 6. Take action. Most people have great ideas combined with great hopes and dreams. However, this is the big killer for most people, because they are procrastinators. Many even get to the point of writing down their goals, but when it comes time to act, they stall—always finding a reason or excuse to procrastinate until a later time.

Step 7. Do something every day to move you toward your major goal. Never let a day go by without performing an action that moves you closer in the direction of what you really want in life. In every study of successful people, it has been found that the most successful are the ones who are action-oriented.

This simple seven-step procedure of deciding exactly what you want, writing it down, setting a deadline, making a list and organizing it into a plan, taking action on the most important item on your list, and then doing something every day towards achieving your goal will change your future in ways you can't even imagine.

On the following page, write your name and today's date, then write down at least ten things you would like to accomplish in the next twelve months. You can write more than ten goals if you like, but you must put a minimum of ten goals on this list.

Be sure to write your goals in the present tense, as though a year has passed and you have already achieved them. For example, if you want to increase your income from $40,000 to $50,000 in the next twelve months, you would write, "I earn $50,000 per year." If you want to lose weight and drop from 180 to 150 pounds, you would write, "I weigh 150 pounds."

When you write a goal in the present tense, it is accepted by your subconscious mind as a command, and your subconscious mind immediately goes to work to bring it into your life.

If you continue to write down your goals and plans and work on them every single day, you will accomplish more in the coming year than you have accomplished in any other year. You will become positive, self-directed, and self-motivated. Your future will become unlimited.

MY GOALS

(Name) _____

1.

2.

3.

4.

5.

6.

7.

8.

9.

10.

Chapter 4

The Wheel of Life—Goal Setting in Each Area of Life

"A well-rounded individual who is balanced and successful in all areas is a person who has not overemphasized one or more dimensions in his life."

A person's lifestyle can be likened to a wheel the rim of which is supported by five vital spokes. If one of the spokes is damaged or weakened, the whole wheel becomes threatened. The five spokes could represent the five key-action areas in your life: physical, mental, spiritual, financial, and social. All are equally important. All demand serious attention by the person determined to break the bounds of imposed limitation.

The five key-action areas form an intricate web supporting a harmonious person. No area can be ignored. Which spoke of a wheel is the most important? The healthy meshing and balancing of all key-action areas develops a well-rounded, successful person capable of continued growth and expansion. Interactions between physical, mental, and spiritual become obvious. The man who neglects his well-being cannot strain during the rigors and challenges of growth. A stunted mental development confines a person to small and simple-minded activity. Spiritual growth, regardless of its nature, helps to provide the initial zest to the challenges of success. Financial endeavors give us life's necessities and deserved luxuries as well as the opportunity to expand our horizons even further. Social contacts add depth, warmth, and responsibility to our personal adventure. It is the sum total of these activities that makes the balanced, well-rounded, successful human being—a human being who will not be denied and who is not denied.

Remember, when setting strategic goals, it is vitally important to have a balanced goal program. Balance means setting goals for achievement in harmony with all five important areas of your life.

A well-rounded individual who is balanced and successful in all areas is a person who hasn't overemphasized one or more dimensions in his life. If he does, he becomes unbalanced and his five points of the strategic goals program get out of balance, become crammed or skewed. Having a short-term tangible goal is the easiest way to begin to establish strategic goals. For example, resolve to lose weight, buy a car, write a letter, fix a door, mow the lawn, or spend more time with the grandchildren. The greatest rewards in life, however, come with the achievement of a long-term intangible goal. For example, develop personal characteristics needed to progress in a chosen field, acquire the knowledge or skills required to become an acknowledged expert in a particular profession, gain wisdom and insight into life's meaning and purpose, or gain total success and happiness with peace of mind.

Physical Action Strategies

It is written in the Old Testament that there are no riches greater than a sound body. We might carry this thought even further, for without a sound body, life itself is threatened. These dangers come in many forms. They may be purely physical, causing unexplainable diseases that require treatment, or they may be self-inflicted threats such as obesity, exhaustion, or simple sluggishness—mental as well as physical—resulting from too little exercise. If we are to function well, physical health is a must.

The old saying, "An ounce of prevention is worth a pound of cure" is important to good health. Physical well-being is something to be built. A dietary regimen is often useful. Sleep must be adequate. Exercise is vital to good physical condition and to the release of emotional pressure. All these areas require more than passive concern.

Mental Action Strategies

"There are but two powers in the world," wrote Napoleon, "the sword and the mind. In the long run, the sword is always beaten by the mind." At first glance, it seems odd that these words came from one of the greatest warriors of Western history; however, by remembering that Napoleon's skills were those of a general—and not a swordsman—his emphasis on the mind becomes natural. It is in the mind where the strategies of battles and history are made, whether they are for a nation or for a single man with direction and purpose. Regardless of occupation or profession, mental alertness, growth, and well-being are key ingredients of personal success and happiness.

Sound mental health reflects positive attitudes and the willingness to act. If you are full of doubt and insecurity, you are beckoning failure. You will picture yourself a failure, and a failure you will be. Even a healthy mind needs continuous food and exercise. It is as prone to weakness from starvation and passivity as any muscle. Effective, meaningful activity requires positive direction. Expansion and growth demand purpose and discipline originating in attitudes. The development of your strategic goals should include mental considerations, whether they are in the form of expanded personal reading programs, occupational knowledge, travel, or some other activity. As you begin outlining this section of your plan, keep in mind these words of the Renaissance genius, Leonardo da Vinci: "Iron rusts from disease; water loses its purity from stagnation and in cold, water becomes frozen; even so does inaction sap the vigors of the day."

Spiritual Action Strategies

The spiritual realm can be a vital element in any person's success. How do you pursue this highly personal spiritual area? That depends on you, but the decision must be made, for the sake of harmony with nature and with your fellow man. When considering your personal success survival strategies plan, allow adequate emphasis for spiritual development. It adds a special sense to life. It gives purpose to many diverse activities. It is a force that builds personal security and self-assurance.

The universality of human spiritual needs was appropriately emphasized by Charles Steinmetz, who was neither a theologian, a philosopher, nor a psychologist, but an electrical engineer. He was a man who fully realized the impact of religion. He wrote, "Spiritual power is a force which history clearly teaches has been the greatest force in the development of man. Yet, we have been merely playing with it and never have really studied it as we have the physical forces."

Social Action Strategies

Humans are by nature gregarious, constantly seeking the companionship of others. They have an insatiable need for love and affection. Their concerns with protection and safety have led them to evolve the most complex social systems imaginable. As you develop your success survival strategies, set your sights on various social activities and accomplishments. Do you desire membership in a particular club? Will new contacts enhance your stature? Can personal rewards be found through specific fraternal or other organizations? Whatever your social goals may be, success is now within your reach.

Financial Action Strategies

When kept within reason, finances play a respectable role in our lives. Norwegian poet and dramatist Henrik Ibsen put it this way: "Money may be the husk of many things, but not the kernel. It brings you food, but not appetite; medicine, but not health; acquaintances, but not friends; servants, but not faithfulness; days of joy, but not peace or happiness."

Now may be the time for a new awareness of your own financial situation. Just where do you stand? Just where do you wish to stand in the future? How much will it take to get you to the goals you have set for yourself? These questions are not meant to create anxiety. On the contrary, now is the time to start planning so that you may have all the things both for yourself and your family. By proper financial management, many of your greatest dreams can become reality. The things you want, you can have through carefully planned goal-oriented money management.

The Baby Boomer Strategy Planner

At the end of this chapter you will find a Baby Boomer Strategy Planner form. The strategy for success follows a simple course. It begins with a process of brainstorming and follows through six other steps:

- Objectives (your top priority goals)
- Primary barriers
- Strategy procedures
- Initiation dates
- Completion dates
- Rewards

To clarify the use of this system, we will comment briefly on each step, so you will be able to easily follow your personal blueprint for achievement.

Brainstorming

By brainstorming, you let your imagination soar without restraint, carrying you to new and expanded heights. List your dreams. Look at the abundant world that surrounds you and ask, "What do I want? What do I wish to achieve? What do I want to be?" Relax. Blast away any inhibitions that block free association. Consider every possible aspect of life's five key-action areas. Don't worry now about what you'll have to do to see your dreams evolve to realities. Just let your mind wander . . . Do you want more education? Then list it in the brainstorming sections. Have you dreamed of foreign travel? A better career? A new home? Nicer clothes? Whatever your dreams, list them on the brainstorming area.

Objectives

After selecting a top-priority objective for each action area, write it in the proper section of the Baby Boomer Strategy Planner in the box labeled "Objectives." Beneath the objective title, write a specific definition and a detailed description of your goal.

Estimate the financial cost involved. For example, if your objective is a new car, decide on the make, the model, the color, and the cost. If it's more education, pinpoint the specific school you wish to attend and find out all you can about it. The reason for all this detail is quite simple: *You must define your objectives before you can reach them.*

Barriers and Strategy Procedures

Unfortunately, life doesn't always proceed as smoothly as we have planned. Whether we like it or not, life offers many more barriers and obstructions than it does easy roads. If obtaining personal achievement and happiness is a general goal, then you must learn to overcome these obstacles. Every person who has done anything successfully has, somewhere along the line, overcome seemingly impossible barriers.

Barriers can be classified as either real or imaginary. Real obstructions are directly concerned with the physical world. They may come in the form of insufficient money to buy those things you want or need or some other real hurdle standing between you and your objective.

On the other hand, our minds create a multitude of imaginary barriers. These are thought-blocks originating in negative attitudes. While real problems usually originate in social relationships, imaginary ones have their beginnings in our relations with *ourselves*. We should always recognize the nature of a barrier. The first step in overcoming a setback is to define it.

Remember that a barrier isn't something to bring your pursuit of happiness to a dead halt. Almost all obstacles can be overcome with a bit of planning. Financial problems, which at first seem incapable of solution, can be solved with imagination. Interpersonal problems can be tackled despite apparently insurmountable difficulties.

A personal success strategy means a study of your objective. List the three most important barriers in the appropriate place on your strategy chart. Finally, devise a step-by-step strategy to overcome those obstacles.

Start Dates and Completion Deadlines

There is a Persian proverb that states: "Thinking well is wise; planning well, wiser; doing well, wisest and best of all." Thus far, the Baby Boomer Strategy Planner exercises have been concerned with thinking and planning. Now it's time to buckle down to the serious business of "doing." We all have a tendency to procrastinate. Given the opportunity, we'll try to delay projects that should be given immediate attention. Your next step is to set specific dates—timelines—to implement pertinent procedures.

Set a starting date for each strategy procedure. This is important. Many people have a tendency to delay the start of a project until immediately before a deadline. The result is often a haphazard completion—if the deadline is met at all. Start dates are vital steps in strategic planning.

Completion deadlines are no different than any other target or objective. They give us something to work toward. They become goals in themselves, curbing delays and getting the task at hand completed on time.

Rewards

The Baby Boomers Survival Handbook has concerned itself with the basic fundamentals of a well-balanced, successful, motivated life, a life unlimited except by your own thoughts and actions. The survival strategies reveal a proven, logical, and simple method that works every time with every person who applies its principles. It is a method that can assure financial success; an expanding intellect; a healthy mental, physical, and spiritual attitude; and esteem, recognition, and admiration.

Define Your Goals

What do you want out of life? Write down the things that you really want to attain, acquire, achieve, or accomplish.

What are your physical goals?

What are your mental goals?

What are your spiritual goals?

What are your social goals?

What are your financial goals?

BABY BOOMER STRATEGY PLANNER

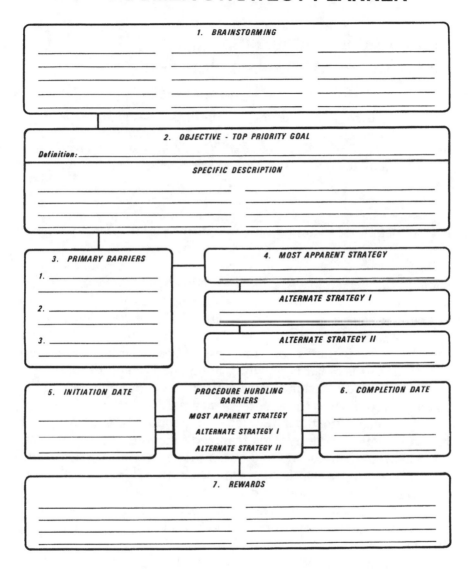

1. BRAINSTORMING

2. OBJECTIVE - TOP PRIORITY GOAL

Definition:

SPECIFIC DESCRIPTION

3. PRIMARY BARRIERS

1.

2.

3.

4. MOST APPARENT STRATEGY

ALTERNATE STRATEGY I

ALTERNATE STRATEGY II

5. INITIATION DATE

PROCEDURE HURDLING BARRIERS

MOST APPARENT STRATEGY

ALTERNATE STRATEGY I

ALTERNATE STRATEGY II

6. COMPLETION DATE

7. REWARDS

Chapter 5

Mental Action Strategies—
Overview of Mental Development

When we exercise our muscles, we know that we keep them toned and healthy. However, when it comes to improving our brain function, we tend to overlook the benefit of brain exercises. Our brain power can be improved by using brain exercises the same as physical exercises for our body.

To begin, let's summarize some of the significant characteristics of the human brain.

The human brain weighs about three to four pounds and is sometimes referred to as the most complex object in the universe. It has over 100 billion neurons linked in a network that gives rise to our consciousness and memory. We may think of the mind as a collection of mental processes rather than a substance or spirit. Therefore, the mind includes consciousness, urges, moods, desires, and conscious forms of learning, which are mental phenomena.

The brain is divided into two hemispheres commonly referred to as the right brain and the left brain. Each part of the brain is responsible for specific functions. Your left brain tends to be responsible for linear, sequential, orderly, and organized functions. It deals with the verbal, the mathematical, and the scientific. The left brain deals with details in a step-by-step fashion in processing information, whereas your right brain is holistic and deals with complete pictures and fully integrated ideas and situations. Creative, musical, and artistic abilities are located in the right brain. Problem solving, decision making, feelings, and intuitive abilities are processed in the right brain. If you learn to harmonize both of these parts of the brain so they work together, you will be able to perform at an exceptional level.

The ability to visualize the self is important in the development of personality and a sense of objectivity. Once this self is established, most people tend to protect it, often by such thought processes as rationalization, inhibition, and projection. A person is better able to visualize the self if he analyzes his status or rank within the group.

The human mind can be compared to a powerful computer that is installed between your ears with the capacity for logic, storage, reasoning, and recall. Although the brain is different from a computer, this analogy can be helpful. The mind has three memory systems: sensory memory, short-term memory (STM), and long-term memory (LTM). Most of our daily memory chores are handled by STM and LTM. STM is like a computer's RAM (random access memory) that quickly evaporates. It can enable you to perform simple calculations in your head or retain phone numbers for a short period of time without creating a lasting memory.

Long-term memory can be compared to a computer's hard drive, which records past experiences in the cerebral cortex. There are over 10 billion nerve cells that communicate by electrical impulse. Anything that activates the network will bring back the original perception as a memory. If things are frequently rehearsed, they become a permanent part of long-term memory. The memory functions best if there is an emotional significance and if it is related to things we already know.

The brain has no muscles and is incapable of movement, but it is the most active organ in our body. With scientific instruments we can watch the electrical waves on a screen as billions of cells fire their charges and fade like an electrical concert in the mind.

Dr. Wilder Penfield, a Canadian neurosurgeon, exposed the cerebral cortex of a patient undergoing brain surgery for epilepsy. Because there are no pain receptors in the brain, only a local anesthesia was used. The patient was awake as electrodes were placed at various locations of the brain. When certain areas were electrically stimulated, the patient began to produce vivid memories of long-forgotten events with sound, smell, and color. These findings led Dr. Penfield to claim that the brain records the past like a continuous strip of movie film complete with soundtrack.

The "brain" has not always been recognized as the location of the mind. The mind means the part of a human being that enables him to know, think, and act effectively. Plato was convinced that the mind was located inside the head. On the other hand, Aristotle believed that the mind was in the heart. René Descartes indicated that the mind was a nonmaterial thing. It might live in the brain but it was separate from the physical tissues found inside the head. In one sense Descartes was correct in that the mind is not a physical object and it exists within the brain at no particular location. However, he was wrong in his assertion that the mind and body are wholly independent. The latest research tends to indicate that the mind is created by the brain.

Scientists are uncovering essential information about how memory works, and new imaging techniques are revealing how different parts of the brain interact. Memory can be defined as an active system that receives, stores, organizes, alters, and recovers information. Neuroscientists continue to learn how stress, age, and other factors can disrupt chemical processes, while biologists decode the essential processes.

It is generally believed that there is a significant decline in mental ability when a person reaches the age of sixty-five or seventy, but this is not always true. In a recent study of some 30 million Americans over the age of sixty-five, only 10 percent showed any significant loss of memory, and fewer than half of those showed any serious mental impairment. The data tend to show that age alone will not destroy your memory, especially your long-term memory. Unless you develop a vascular disease or Alzheimer's, when you become a senior citizen you will still be able to encode information with very little decline in memory.

Dementia and the Aging Baby Boomer

Dementia, whether it occurs in late adulthood or earlier, is a serious memory loss. The most common cause of dementia is Alzheimer's disease.

One form of dementia is caused by a series of mini-strokes that occur when impairment of blood circulation destroys part of the brain tissue. Measures to improve circulation and to control hypertension can prevent or slow the course of this form of dementia. Other organic causes of dementia are brain tumors, Parkinson's disease, and Down's Syndrome. Some mental problems that are frequently misdiagnosed as dementia include drug misuse, alcohol abuse, and psychological illness.

Baby Boomers and Alzheimer's Disease

In a recent survey of the major concerns of Baby Boomers, the fear of developing Alzheimer's disease or of their parents developing Alzheimer's was at the top of the list. Thus, in our overview of mental development, a summary of scientific findings on Alzheimer's disease may be useful.

While some cases of Alzheimer's are genetic, for the most part the cause is unknown. It is considered the most devastating of all diseases because it affects our ability to remember and to think clearly. It is estimated that approximately 9 million Americans will have Alzheimer's by the year 2040.

The most characteristic early symptoms of Alzheimer's is the gradual onset of short-term memory loss—difficulty remembering names, recent events, and conversations; misplacing items; missing appointments, and repeating comments or questions. This age-associated memory impairment usually does not interfere with social or occupational activities.

Patients with Alzheimer's exhibit an inability to learn new skills and information. They react more slowly and lack initiative, spontaneity, and insight into their deficits. In addition, judgment, problem-solving, and visual-spatial skills are impaired, and difficulty in finding the right word may begin to occur with increasing regularity. Personality and behavioral changes are present.

Remote memory, past well-learned information, and social skills usually are retained early in the disease. In the mid-stage of the disease, patients become disoriented, have worsening language difficulties, and short- and long-term memory loss. They lose the ability to calculate and may develop suspiciousness, delusions, hallucinations, and other mental disorders.

Techniques for Memory Improvement

With a little practice, you should be able to greatly improve your memory. Practice using the following techniques:

Use mental pictures. There are at least two kinds of memory, *visual* and *verbal*. Visual pictures or images are generally easier to remember than words. Turning information into mental pictures is therefore very helpful.

Make things meaningful. Transferring information from short-term to long-term memory is aided by making it meaningful. If you encounter technical terms that have little or no immediate meaning for you, give them meaning even if you have to stretch the term to do so.

Make information familiar. Connect it to what you already know. Another way to get information into long-term memory is to connect it to information already stored there. If some facts or ideas seem to stay in your memory easily, associate other more difficult facts with them.

Form bizarre, unusual, or exaggerated mental associations. When associating two ideas, terms, or mental images, you will find that the more outrageous and exaggerated the association, the more likely you are to remember it later.

Improving Memory through Brain Exercises

When we exercise our muscles, we know that we keep them toned and healthy. However, when it comes to improving our brain function, we tend to overlook the benefit of brain exercises. Our brain power can be improved by using brain exercises the same as physical exercises for our body.

As you grow older, the formation of neural connections slows down. Neural connections that are used frequently become stronger while those that are not used are lost. When you use your brain, you build nerve circuits. The more circuits you have, the less memory loss you will have over time. Since our mental skills depend on the complexity of the neural connections, we can increase these connections by performing mental calisthenics. Some of the brain exercises that you can perform include such things as crossword puzzles, Scrabble, chess, or bridge. Solve word and number games and games called brain teasers. Read books that challenge you. Other ways to improve your brain power include listening to classical music, learning to play a musical instrument, taking classes, or studying a new language. Engage in frequent social interactions and conversations because they are also brain exercises. If you don't have a hobby, it's a good idea to develop one or volunteer your service to some worthwhile cause.

While you exercise your brain, remember to exercise your body on a regular basis. Physical exercise increases the blood flow to your brain, which raises the level of dopamine in the brain. This causes you to feel good all over.

Memory and Nutrients

Learning and memory are cognitive functions that occur in the brain. Like any other organ in the body, the brain requires fuel and other energizers as additives. Therefore, many doctors and mental health professionals have recommended supplements to help improve the mental functioning of their patients. A healthy mind and a healthy body are essential for you to function properly.

If you want to prevent illness and keep your brain healthy, you must take the initiative and make sure that you keep your brain well nourished. Scientists have recently concluded that nearly every problem with brain functioning can be traced to a chemical or nutrient imbalance. They have isolated vital nutrients that feed the critically important nourishment to the nearly 100 billion neurons (brain cells) that we each have. Without these nutrients, we would have memory loss or more serious problems. As we age, the amount of nutrients that our bodies produce decreases. Without nutrients, neurons die and our memory and thinking capacities diminish.

Therefore, when brain function begins to decline, there is usually a neurotransmitter problem that can almost always be traced to a lack of vital nutrients. Here is a list of some of the supplements found to be valuable in improving cognitive function:

Acetyl L-Carnitine (ALC) is an amino acid that plays a major role in normal brain function. It has been shown to prevent the brown fat accumulation that collects on neurons and prevents transmission of signals from one cell to another.

Ginkgo biloba is a vasodilator (opens blood vessels for faster flow). Study after study has shown that it has enormous value in brain function. *Ginkgo biloba* contains an enzyme, superoxide dismutase (SOD), which can capture free radicals and help prevent lipid peroxidation, one of the brain's foremost enemies. Ginkgo has been used successfully to delay mental deterioration for those suffering from Alzheimer's disease, and used to arrest memory loss that is not age-related.

Phosphatidylserine is a large lipid molecule found in trace amounts in lecithin, which is derived from soybeans. Studies have shown that nutritional supplementation with phosphatidylserine enhances brain functions that tend to decline with age.

Four amino acids, *tyrosine, glutamine, cysteine,* and *phenylalanine,* are vital to brain function. *Tyrosine* has been shown in numerous studies to help relieve depression.

Choline has a significant effect on the structure and functioning of neuronal membranes and brain neurotransmission, producing some charges that are important in memory alteration.

Lecithin/Choline is the major source of the neurotransmitter acetylcholine that determines human behavior. Nerve and brain cells in particular need large quantities of acetylcholine for repair and maintenance. As you age, the production of acetylcholine declines, which leads to a reduction in both short- and long-term memory.

Vitamin E is a fat-soluble antioxidant. By preventing the oxidation of important molecules in cells, it slows down the aging process and improves the memory.

B-Complex vitamins are essential for all aspects of your nervous system including proper mental functioning.

Vitamin C (ascorbic acid) is a key antioxidant and is necessary for the manufacture of neurotransmitters and cell structures.

DHEA (dehydroepiandrosterone) is considered a powerful tool for improvement and maintenance of brain function.

Pregnenolone is one of the most potent memory-enhancing agents yet found. Neurosteroids, which are derived from pregnenolone, seem to facilitate all aspects of brain function.

Memory and Prescription Medications

Eldepryl has been called the basic psycho-energizer because it protects the brain cells that make dopamine.

Hydergine has been shown in study after study to increase intelligence in such mental abilities as learning, memory, and recall.

Dilantin is used primarily as a medicine to prevent seizures. Concentration, intelligence, learning, memory, and verbal performance all improve with use of Dilantin.

If you try any of these intelligence-enhancing substances, always do so under the care of a physician.

EXERCISE 5.1—A Memory Test[1]

Write in the correct number of points for each question.

1 point	Not within the last six months
2 points	Once or twice in the last six months
3 points	About once a month
4 points	About once a week
5 points	Daily
6 points	More than once a day

_____ How often do you fail to recognize places you've been before?

_____ How often do you forget whether you did something, such as lock the door or turn off your computer?

_____ How often do you forget when something happened—wondering whether it was yesterday or last week?

_____ How often do you forget where you put items like your house keys or your glasses?

_____ How often do you forget something you were told recently and have to be reminded of it?

_____ How often are you unable to remember a word or name, even though it's "on the tip of your tongue"?

_____ In conversation, how often do you forget what you were just talking about?

Add up your score: _____ *Score*

7–14   = *Better than average*
15–25   = *Average*
26 or higher = *Below average*

---

[1]Adapted from a test appearing in *Newsweek* magazine on June 15, 1998.

BABY BOOMER STRATEGY PLANNER

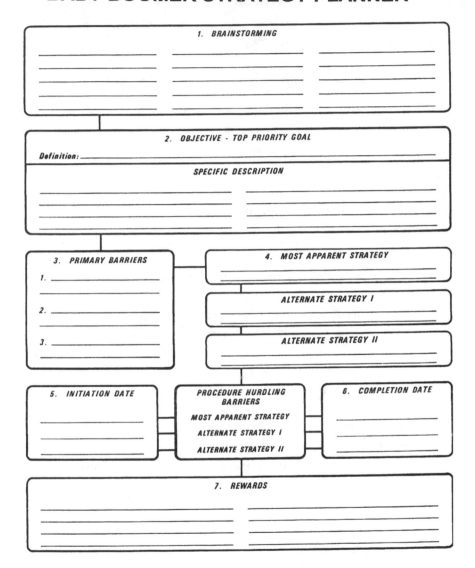

Chapter 6

Developing a Success Psychology
for the Twenty-First Century

The ability to set goals and make plans for their accomplishment is the single most important skill that you can learn and perfect. Becoming an expert at goal setting is something that you absolutely must do if you wish to fulfill your potential as a human being.

One good definition of success refers to the progressive realization of a worthwhile goal. If you are moving towards a predetermined goal according to this definition, you will be successful. Let's look again at goal setting.

Goal Setting—Mastering the Skills of Success

The ability to set goals and make plans for their accomplishment is the single most important skill that you can learn and perfect. Becoming an expert at goal setting is something that you absolutely must do if you wish to fulfill your potential as a human being. Goals enable you to do the work you want to do, to live where you want to live, to be with the people you enjoy, and to become the kind of person you want to become. There is no limit to the financial rewards you can obtain. All you have to do is to set a goal for financial success, make a plan, and then work on the plan until you succeed in that area.

The degree to which you feel in control of your life will largely determine your level of mental well-being, your peace of mind, your happiness, and the quality of your interactions with people. Cognitive psychologists call this a "sense of control." It is the foundation of happiness and high achievement. The only thing in the world over which you have complete control is the content of your conscious mind. If you decide to exert that control and keep your

mind on what you want, even when you are surrounded by difficult circumstances, your future potential will be unlimited.

Your thoughts, whatever they are, trigger mental pictures and
emotions that lead to your saying and doing certain things that are
consistent with those thoughts. With regard to success, when you
think of what success means to you or think about being a great success in your career, you'll think about the things you want to achieve
and you'll feel the pleasure of achieving them. You will begin to take
actions that will lead to the success that you desire. The starting
point is always to think like a winner. Your feelings will trigger
thoughts and mental pictures that will lead to certain actions. For
example, when you feel positive and optimistic, you will smile and
be cheerful. You will be more animated and energetic. You will tend
to be more enthusiastic and more efficient and effective in the things
you do. Your positive feelings will trigger positive responses at all
levels, and your world will be a more positive place. You will attract
positive people and positive circumstances into your life.

To achieve your goals, it is most important to "get the feeling"
that you would have if the goal were already achieved. This is another way of saying if you can create the state of emotion consistent
with the goal and lifestyle that you wish to attain, you will create a
force field of energy that attracts what you want into your life.

Take every opportunity you can to surround yourself with images of what success means to you: get brochures of new cars, get
magazines containing pictures of beautiful homes, beautiful
clothes, and all the other possessions that you will acquire as soon
as you achieve success. Each time you see or visualize those images,
you trigger thoughts, feelings, and actions that make them materi-
alize into your life.

This is another way of saying that your inner impressions will
motivate you to achieve your goals. Your actions will trigger
thoughts, emotions, and images consistent with them. It is one of
the most important success principles ever discovered.

In her book, *Wake Up and Live,* Dorothea Brande said that the most
important success secret she ever discovered was this: "Act as if it
were impossible to fail, and it shall be." She went on to explain that
you need to be very clear about the success that you desire, and then
simply act as if you already have it. Act as if your success is inevitable. Act as if your achievement is guaranteed. Act as if there is

no possibility of failure. You are responsible in a large measure for the things that are happening to you.

Your thoughts are powerful. They have the power to raise and lower your blood pressure, pulse rate, and respiratory rate. They can affect your digestion. If your thoughts are strong enough, they can make you sick or healthy. Your thoughts tend to trigger images in your mind, and those images trigger feelings in your body that are consistent with them. If you think happy and healthy thoughts, you will experience happy and healthy emotions.

Since the human mind has been compared to a computer, there is a humorous formula used by computer programmers that illustrates some of the maladjusted behavior we learn. The formula is GI = GO—Garbage In equals Garbage Out. If you don't program a computer properly, or you don't put the right information into it, you can't expect to get the right information from it. The same is true of your mind.

The Two Components of Your Mind

There are two components of your mind—the conscious mind and the subconscious mind. We use our conscious mind to do our rational thinking and deductive reasoning during the hours we are awake. On the other hand, the subconscious is always busy maintaining our involuntary functions beneath the surface of our conscious thinking. Even while our body and conscious mind are sleeping, our subconscious mind continues to work.

The conscious mind is associated with intelligence, the five senses, voluntary functioning, and decision making. The subconscious is associated with involuntary functioning, feelings, psychic abilities, and the ability to restructure reality. These two components of our mind have respective limitations, which complement each other.

Research studies show that the subconscious mind is not the reasoning part of the mind but will accept thoughts or ideas that penetrate to the subconscious level. It has been compared to good soil that accepts any seed it is given, good or bad, and will then proceed to grow whatever has been planted. Therefore, you may plant positive seeds in your subconscious just as easily as you may plant negative or harmful seeds or thoughts. "As you sow, so shall you reap." Many people have heard this biblical statement most of their lives, but they may not understand how to apply this to their subconscious mind. This is a spiritual law that has been proved to be psychologically sound.

The subconscious mind accepts whatever thoughts are impressed upon it. We develop our self-concept or self-image based on what has been programmed into the subconscious mind from childhood. Because the subconscious mind controls the conscious level of thinking, action frequently takes place without consultation with the conscious mind, but no action ever takes place without reference to the subconscious. Information fed into your subconscious memory bank stays there. The billions of separate items of input over a lifetime are all there awaiting retrieval. They can never be willfully erased by you. They can be overridden or modified, but you are stuck with them for life.

You may believe you are the master of your own destiny, but actually you are a servant to your self-image. Your self-image is the sum total of what you really believe about yourself, and your self-image is controlled by your subconscious. To a certain extent, we all have been programmed since birth.

During every moment of our lives, we program our subconscious mind to work for us or against us. Since it is only a mechanism having no judging function, it strives to meet the objectives and goals we set for it, regardless of whether they are positive or negative, true or false, right or wrong, safe or dangerous. Its sole function is to follow instructions based upon previous inputs.

You are a slave to your subconscious mind, which houses your all-important self-image. If you try to make a change in yourself at the conscious level by using willpower, the change will only be temporary. Any permanent change in your personality or behavior should first involve a change in your self-image, reinforced by a change in your lifestyle. Then your long-range behavior or performance will follow.

How is our self-concept developed and how does it control our behavior? First of all, we must understand that self-concept is not something that we are born with. It is something that is learned and developed in the early years of life. A simple way of understanding how the self-concept is internalized can be illustrated by the diagram referred to as the Johari Window.

JOHARI WINDOW:

	Known to Self	*Unknown to Self*
Known to others:	Public (1)	Blind (2)
Unknown to others:	Private (3)	Subconscious (4)

Explanation: (1) There is one side of us that is known to ourselves and unknown to others. (2) There is another side that is known to others but is unknown or blind to ourselves. Example: A person who works with you may be able to predict your behavior, such as the fact that you always have a cigarette while drinking coffee and you may be unaware of this habit. (3) There is another side of us that is known to ourselves but unknown to others unless you tell them about your innermost secrets such as marital problems, your sex life, and other secrets. (4) There is also another side that is unknown to self and unknown to others, but this subconscious side determines most of our outward behavior.

When people say positive or negative things to us, it is the subconscious mind that is becoming conditioned. It is because of our subconscious that many people find it hard to break old habits such as smoking and losing weight.

In order to change behaviors or ideas that have been programmed into the subconscious mind, we can use several techniques that have been successful in changing the stored memories. Hypnosis is one such technique, while self-affirmation is probably the most frequently used technique to change behavior or memories stored in the subconscious. This procedure requires that you repeat positive affirmations to yourself over and over until you replace certain negative thoughts with positive ones.

Affirmations are based on the three Ps:

Positive Statements—"I like myself."
Personal Statements—"I am responsible."
First Person Present Tense—"I feel terrific."

It is important that you tell yourself, "I am . . . " rather than "I will . . . " because the subconscious responds only to the present tense, not to past or future tense. You should make up specific affirmations to go along with the characteristics you want to develop. This technique has been found to be very powerful if the affirmations are said with conviction and belief. Through the power of suggestion, we are able to change our negative habits. These techniques must involve other sensory forms such as visualization, hearing, taste, touch, and emotions.

If the affirmations are repeated in the morning and late at night just before going to bed or when you meditate, then you are most susceptible to the implanting of new data into your subconscious mind. The EEG (electroencephalograph), which measures brain wave patterns, shows that when a person is awake and alert, short waves called beta waves appear, whereas, immediately before sleep, a different pattern of waves occur called alpha waves. Alpha waves occur when a person is more relaxed, when breathing becomes slow and regular, the pulse rate and body temperature drops, all of which makes us more susceptible to the power of suggestion.

The use of visualization creates a mental picture of the person you want to be, and you see yourself doing the things you want to do. Your subconscious goes to work to bring change about. People sometimes have a tendency to disbelieve the power of affirmations, but the more you say them and the more you visualize them, then disbelief changes to belief.

Six Steps to Change Your Self-Concept

The following steps are necessary in order to change your self-concept:

Desire—You must have the desire or an intense need to change.

Belief—It is very important that you believe you can change.

Action—Once you have decided what you want and what you hope to achieve, you must take action and you must practice.

Feedback—When you practice, you are going to make mistakes. It is important to correct the information that you feed into your subconscious mind.

Repetition—It is necessary to perform the behavior over and over until it become a habit. You should use all sensory forms.

Self-Discipline—Repetition requires self-discipline, which underlies all new habit patterns, physical or mental. You will need to practice this new behavior for at least thirty days. After repeated practice, the new behavior will become a habit.

Remember:

- The self constitutes your picture of yourself. Most of the behaviors that you adopt are those that are consistent with your self-concept.
- You are susceptible to the power of suggestion from your relatives, teachers, co-workers, peers, newspapers, books, television, and the Internet—literally from everyone and everything with which you come into contact.
- Your beliefs influence your reality. To change your reality, you must change your thinking because the way you think regulates the way you act. The first step toward a new way of thinking, toward a brighter, more positive life, is to begin identifying with mental pictures that lift you up.
- You won't break old, unwanted habits by denying or stopping them; you will do it by substituting more positive and productive ones in their place.
- Change only one behavior at a time. After practicing your new behavior for thirty days, you may then want to identify another habit you want to change.
- Belief is the key. It is the launching pad from which your journey to a new life begins. The stronger the emotion, the more powerful is the transmission of the thought patterns.

Seven Mental Laws

We live in an orderly universe in which everything happens for a reason. Just as there are physical laws, there are mental and spiritual laws. These laws are undetectable to the eye. However, we can witness their results. For example, the spiritual law "whatsoever a man soweth, that shall he also reap," means that whatever you send out in words or deeds will return to you. As we move into the twenty-first century, the law of cause and effect may be summarized as learning and doing. You will be rewarded on the basis of your knowledge and know-how, and your ability to apply your knowledge and know-how to improve the lives of other people.

Seven of the most important mental laws are listed here. (Tracy, 1996)

Law of Attraction—According to this law, you are a living magnet—you invariably attract people into your life who harmonize with your dominant thoughts and emotions. The people in your life are there because you have attracted them by the person you are, by the thoughts you hold, and by the emotions you experience. If you are unhappy with the people surrounding you, you are responsible. You have attracted them and you are keeping them there.

Law of Cause and Effect—More than 400 years before Christ, Socrates espoused a basic law of human life. It states that for every effect in your life, there is a cause. If there is any effect that you desire, you can trace it back to the cause and by duplicating the cause, you can have the effect.

Law of Correspondence—This law states that everything that is happening to you on the outside is due to something that is happening to you on the inside. As soon as you look within yourself, you begin to see things that you had completely missed when you were busy blaming others and making excuses.

Law of Belief—According to this law, whatever you believe with feelings or strong emotions becomes your reality.

Law of Expectation—This law states that your self-fulfilling prophecy develops as a result of whatever you expect with confidence.

Law of Mental Equivalency—According to this law, your thoughts, visually imagined and represented, charged with emotion, become your reality.

Law of Control—This law states that you feel positive about yourself to the extent that you are in control of your life.

EXERCISE 6.1 —The Baby Boomers Strategic Planner

What would you do, where would you go, and how would you spend your time if you learned that you had only six months to live from today's date?

1. _____

2. _____

3. _____

What three great things would you do if you knew you could not fail?

1. _____

2. _____

3. _____

What would you do and how would you change your life if you won $1 million cash in a lottery tomorrow?

1. _____

2. _____

3. _____

List six positive affirmations you plan to repeat to yourself several times a day in order to change your behavior.

1. _____

2. _____

3. _____

4. _____

5. _____

6. _____

List the ten most important tasks facing you at the present time.

1. _____

2. _____

3. _____

4. _____

5. _____

6. _____

7. _____

8. _____

9. _____

10. _____

List the three most important tasks from the ten above.

1. _____

2. _____

3. _____

Chapter 7

Interaction of Mind and Body— Coping with Stress

A certain level of stress is important to our well-being. It can motivate us for action for fast decision making and when dealing with emergencies.

What Exactly Is Stress?

In simple terms, stress can be defined as the rate of wear and tear that occurs within the body. It can be classified as the body's non-specific response to any demand placed on it. Any behavior that we are involved in causes stress of some sort—good or bad. It should be noted early on that not all stress is "bad stress." A certain level of stress is important to our well-being. It can motivate us for action for fast decision making and when dealing with emergencies.

Eons ago, our bodies automatically responded with an inborn protective mechanism that helped our ancestors survive when they met danger. This protective mechanism is sometimes called the fight or flight response. We are still programmed to respond to threats and dangers the same way, but in our civilized society we have to suppress that response. When we do that over a period of time, the bottled-up stress begins to cause problems such as fatigue, tension, worry, distraction, and the large assortment of other symptoms and illnesses. When you are under stress, your pituitary gland releases hormones that trigger certain reactions such as the release of adrenaline. The pupils of your eyes become dilated and your body tenses up, preparing for fight or flight.

In an article appearing in the *New York Times* on October 13, 1998, it was stated that "Chronic stress sets into motion a cascade of biological events involving scores of chemicals in the body . . . Such stress lowers resistance and alters gene expression. When people are under stress, wounds tend to heal more slowly, latent viruses like herpes erupt and brain cells involved in memory formation die off."

In the same article, the question was asked, "But what about the opposite? Can a thought or belief produce a chemical cascade that leads to healing and wellness? Researchers studying placebos think the answer is yes."

After a stressful event, your body needs time to recover and return to normal and rebuild all of the lost resources. When you don't give your body a chance to recuperate, you deplete these resources. The effect of constant stress will begin to trigger tension headaches and a variety of physical symptoms. Sometimes you will adapt by ignoring the discomfort and danger signals. Physical symptoms such as pain, high blood pressure, and other intense symptoms are signals for you to start concentrating on finding ways to cope with the stress.

One major cause of stress is worry. It is a form of fear that can result in indecision. Indecisiveness can lead to negative stress that will cause a part of your brain to shut down and prevent you from attaining your goals. There are usually two kinds of worries the first is about problems we can solve, and the second is about problems beyond our ability to personally solve.

Baby Boomers and Stress

In a recent survey of more than ten thousand Baby Boomers, 85% described their mental health as excellent or good. Yet anxiety and depression are not uncommon: 18% reported they often suffer from anxiety, while 14% said they have suffered from depression in the last year.

More than four in ten respondents (43%) reported experiencing stress often. The employed are much more stressed than the retired (49% vs. 20%). Nearly half of those surveyed (46%) indicated that they are trying to relieve stress, and 91% agreed that mental stress can cause physical ailments. Seven in ten of the respondents (70%) said that mental stress wears them out more than physical activity.

Four out of ten (40%) of those who suffer from stress identified the major cause of their distress as "financial concerns." This was followed by "family problems."

How do Baby Boomers deal with stress? Talking with friends is the most common method, but there are gender and age differences in the way people cope with their stress. Women, for example, say they talk with family rather than friends and men say they watch TV to relieve stress. Older respondents (those over fifty) are the least likely to talk with friends, preferring to watch TV to get rid of stress.

Below, we have listed some of the most common symptoms and illnesses that have been attributed to stress. The fact that there are so many symptoms and illnesses indicates just how serious stress can be.

Physical Problems Caused by Stress

Alcoholism
Arthritis
Asthma
Backaches
Cancer
Cardiac arrhythmias
Colitis
Coronary heart disease
Dermatitis
Diarrhea
Dietary problems (includes overeating, skipping meals, etc.)
Duodenal and gastric ulcers
Fatigue
Headaches (migraine and tension)
High cholesterol
Hypertension
Immune system dysfunctions
Indigestion
Infections (frequent)

Muscle aches/muscle weakness
Nausea and vomiting (frequent)
Pain without physical cause
Palpitations
Premenstrual tension
Sciatica
Sleep problems (insomnia/oversleeping)
Tension headaches
Urination (frequent)

Psychological or Social Problems Caused by Stress

Absenteeism or tardiness (frequent)
Argumentative behavior
Boredom
Car accidents or near misses
Chronic anger
Compulsions
Depersonalization
Depression
Dread of getting out of bed
Drug use and dependence
Impaired judgment
Panic disorders
Phobias
Rigidity
Road rage
Sexual dysfunctions
Smoking
Social withdrawal
Suicide attempts
Tearfulness
Trauma

Getting Rid of Stress

One of the best techniques for getting rid of stress is to follow the outlined four step-program:

Step 1. Define the problem.
Step 2. Write down the very worst thing that could possibly happen.
Step 3. Accept the worst that could happen should it ever occur.
Step 4. Take action to prevent the worst possible thing from happening.

Stress can be precipitated by having too many activities in your life. Setting clear goals and listing them by priority will help you arrange your time. Select the most valuable thing you could be doing and concentrate on that one task until it is complete. You can use this method to create positive stress and improve your overall effectiveness and performance.

Progressive Relaxation

Progressive relaxation refers to a method in which people learn to relax systematically, completely, and by choice. The basic idea is to tighten all the muscles in a given area of the body (the arm for instance) and then voluntarily relax them. By tensing and relaxing each area of the body, it is possible, with practice, to greatly reduce tension.

To begin this technique, take a deep breath, then release it. Tense the muscles in your right arm until they tremble. Hold them tight for about five seconds and then let go. Allow your hand and arm to go limp and to relax completely. Take a deep breath. Repeat the procedure.

Releasing tension two or three times will allow you to feel whether or not your arm muscles have relaxed. Repeat the tension-release procedure with your left arm. Take a deep breath. Repeat until the left arm is equally relaxed.

Apply the progressive relaxation technique to your right leg, to your left leg, to your abdomen, to your chest, and to your shoulders. Clench and release your chin, neck, and throat. Wrinkle and release your forehead and scalp. Tighten and release your mouth and face muscles. As a last step, curl your toes and tense your feet. Then release.

Practice relaxation with this method until you can achieve complete relaxation quickly (within 5 to 10 minutes). While relaxed, visualize a beautiful vacation spot with your eyes closed. Play a CD or tape with some soft music.

After you have practiced relaxation once a day for a week or two, you will begin to be able to tell when your body (or a group of muscles) is tense. Also you will begin to be able to relax on command. The visualization will help induce your body to secrete endorphins that will counteract the negative effects of stress.

Social and Psychological Ways of Coping with Stress

- Be flexible
- Schedule in relaxation time
- Create environments that reduce stress
- Delegate work, chores, and responsibilities
- Develop a plan and a goal
- Don't procrastinate
- Don't say yes to everything
- Establish a routine
- Face reality and choose options that are realistic
- Improve interpersonal skills, treat people like human beings
- Know your values and be aware of your strengths and weaknesses
- Leave time for the unexpected
- Maintain a sense of humor
- Seek spiritual nourishment
- Take control of your life by organizing your schedule and commitments
- Use modern technology to save time and effort
- Ventilate, release anger appropriately

Physical Ways of Coping with Stress

- Avoid hypoglycemia (low blood sugar)
- Avoid vitamin depletion
- Employ biofeedback and imaging techniques
- Get plenty of rest and exercise
- Monitor salt intake
- Practice progressive muscle relaxation
- Recognize early signs of stress illness and get treated

EXERCISE 7.1—Self-Observable Signs of Stress

In the following chart, put a check mark by the signs of stress that apply to you:

Physical Signs of Stress

_____ Pounding of the heart
_____ Dryness of the throat or mouth
_____ Feelings of weakness or dizziness
_____ Excessive or chronic fatigue not related to physical exertion
_____ Episodes of trembling or nervous tics
_____ Tendency to be easily startled by small sounds, etc.
_____ Insomnia (being unable to fall asleep, waking up frequently throughout the night)
_____ Wanting to sleep too much
_____ Frequently having bad dreams or nightmares
_____ Sweating
_____ The need to urinate frequently
_____ Diarrhea, indigestion, queasiness in the stomach and sometimes even vomiting
_____ Migraine headaches

_____ Pain in the neck or lower back

_____ Loss of appetite

_____ Constant eating of snacks, even when you aren't hungry

_____ Increased smoking

_____ Increased consumption of alcoholic beverages

_____ Increased use of legally prescribed drugs, such as tranquilizers, headache remedies, etc.

_____ Alcohol or drug addiction

Psychological/Social Signs of Stress

_____ General irritability, hyperexcitation, or depression

_____ Impulsive behavior

_____ The overpowering urge to cry or run and hide

_____ Inability to concentrate

_____ General disorientation

_____ Loss of "joie de vivre" (joy of life)

_____ "Floating anxiety"—being afraid, although you don't know exactly what you are afraid of

_____ Emotional tension—feeling of being "keyed up"

EXERCISE 7.2—How Much Stress Is in Your Life?

Instructions: Think of what has happened to you in the past year as you read through the Stress Test below. Write down the point values for each event that applies to you in the blank column, then add up your score. Keep in mind that major stress events usually come in groups. For example, using the scale below, a divorce (73 points) is often accompanied by a change in residence (20 points). The actual physical separation may be preceded by a change in the number of marital arguments (35 points). Thus, a single event, such as divorce, can actually be an assortment of events, with a value in excess of 125 points. (Holmes and Rahe, 1967)

Life Event	Point Value	Your Score (insert point values from previous column)
Death of spouse	100	
Divorce	73	
Marital separation	65	
Death of close family member	63	
Personal injury or illness	53	
Marriage	50	
Fired at work	47	
Marital reconciliation	45	
Retirement	45	
Change in health of family member	44	
Pregnancy	40	
Sex difficulties	39	
Gain of new family member	39	
Business readjustment	39	
Change in financial status	38	
Death of a close friend	37	
Change to a different line of work	36	
Change in number of arguments with spouse	35	
Mortgage over $100,000	31	
Foreclosure of mortgage or loan	30	
Change in responsibilities at work	29	
Son or daughter leaving home (for college, their own apartment, etc.)	29	

(continued)

Adult son or daughter returning home to live	29	
Trouble with parents or in-laws	29	
Outstanding personal achievement	28	
Spouse begins or stops work	28	
Change in living conditions	25	
Revision of personal habits	24	
Trouble at work with boss or supervisor	23	
Change in work hours or conditions	20	
Change in residence	20	
Change in recreational activities	19	
Change in church activities	18	
Change in social activities	18	
Mortgage less than $100,000	17	
Change in sleep habits	16	
Change in number of family get-togethers	15	
Change in eating habits (starting diet, etc.)	15	
Vacation	13	
Christmas	12	
Minor violations of the law	11	

Total score for the previous 12 months _____

BABY BOOMER STRATEGY PLANNER

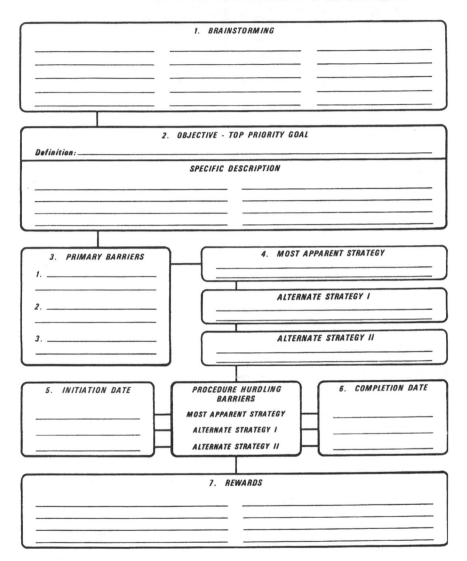

Interpreting Your Score: If your total for the previous year is under 150, you probably won't have any adverse physical reaction. A score of 150–200 indicates a "mild" problem. You stand a good chance of feeling the impact of stress in your life with physical symptoms. If you scored between 200 and 300, you qualify as having a "moderate" problem. If your score is over 300, you have a 90% chance of becoming physically ill as a result of the added stress in your life. Obviously the higher your score, the more cautious you should be about tackling additional life changes.

Chapter 8

Physical Action Strategies

You must have a positive state of mind in order to bring harmony to the body. The body (lifestyle), spirit (desire), and mind (belief) must come together if you are to have better health.

A mericans are living longer, but they aren't living healthier. In a national sample of 1,752 men and women over eighteen years of age, the findings were as follows: (*Parade*, 1998)

- Two-thirds of Americans surveyed say they are in excellent or good health, yet one in five is afraid to go to the doctor.
- The majority say they would prefer to change their diets to treat a health problem, rather than take medication.
- Almost two-thirds of Americans currently take medications, with 49% taking prescription drugs and 30% using over-the-counter medications.
- Half of Americans do not exercise—but 87% of them say that they should.
- Ninety-two percent of those surveyed have medical insurance— for 57% it's managed care.
- Sterilization is the most popular form of birth control, chosen by 29%.
- More women than men go to doctors.
- Assisted suicide is supported by two-thirds of those surveyed.
- Sixteen percent of Americans have sought help from mental health professionals, but 59% of those surveyed have no faith in them.

- Americans are most concerned about having enough money or insurance to pay for a major illness or operation (49%) or for long-term care (46%).
- Forty-three percent of Americans self-medicate to avoid paying for a visit to the doctor.

Our Top Ten Health Problems

The most common health problem cited by survey respondents is arthritis—25% of those surveyed say they have it. Women suffer from arthritis more than men (31% vs. 20%) and the likelihood rises with age (54% of those age sixty-five and older). High blood pressure comes in next, affecting 23%. Both sexes are equally affected and it also increases with age, from 8% of those age eighteen to thirty-four to 49% of those age sixty-five and older.

Depression is the third most common disease reported by the survey respondents—14% say they became depressed in the last year (17% of the women and 10% of the men). In this case, the incidence is lowest among those sixty-five and older.

Asthma affects 9% of the survey respondents—more women (11%) than men (7%). Next comes cancer. About 8% of those surveyed—equal numbers of men and women—report having had some form of the disease other than skin cancer. The incident of cancer also increases with age, from 2% of those age eighteen to thirty-four to 23% of those age sixty-five and older.

Seven percent of respondents have heart disease with slightly more women (8%) reporting this problem than men (6%). The incidence of heart disease rises from less than 1% of those age eighteen to thirty-four to 22% of those age sixty-five and older.

Six percent of the respondents have diabetes, which affects both sides equally. Five percent report that they suffer from an anxiety disorder with the rate higher among women (7%) than men (4%). Finally, 4% of the respondents have skin cancer, and 4% cite alcoholism as a personal health problem. (Parade, 1998)

Our Greatest Fears

Obesity is the number-one public health problem in America today. Americans may be watching what they eat, but the real issue is controlling the amount of food they put on their plates and becoming more active. When asked, "What is your greatest personal concern for the future?," the largest number of respondents (16%) said "cancer"; 15% said "heart problems" and 12% said "weight."

Older and Wiser

Eating and health habits improve with age—77% of those age sixty-five and older describe their eating habits as "excellent" or "good" compared with 53% of those between the ages of eighteen and twenty-four.

The Top Ten Killers

1. Disease of the heart
2. Cancer
3. Stroke
4. Chronic lung diseases
5. Accidents
6. Pneumonia and flu
7. Diabetes
8. HIV infection
9. Suicide
10. Chronic liver disease and cirrhosis

Normal Changes in Middle Adulthood

Between the ages of forty and sixty, aging continues at the same steady rate, but the levels of physical change that are now reached are more difficult to ignore. Adults in middle age can do a great deal to safeguard their vitality and compensate for many of the physiological declines they experience, discovering that though aging is inevitable, it is not inevitably bad.

What We Fear Now	What We Fear in the Future
Weight	Heart problems
Cancer	Weight
Heart problems	Staying healthy
High blood pressure	High blood pressure
Arthritis	
High cholesterol	

As Baby Boomers advance in age past forty, they will begin to notice that their hair starts to turn gray and thins, their skin becomes drier and more wrinkled, and their body shape changes, as "middle-age spread" develops and pockets of fat settle on various other parts of the body. Overeating and underexercising will result in more weight gain. As back muscles, connecting tissues, and bones lose strength, the vertebrae may collapse somewhat, causing a loss of nearly an inch in height by age sixty.

In general, these changes in appearance may not result in significant health problems. The consequences for self-image, however, can be significant, especially for women because of the cultural link between youthful beauty, sexual attractiveness, and social status, which is much stronger for women than for men.

Because the aging process is so gradual, especially if you are a fit and healthy Baby Boomer, a number of years may pass without your giving much thought to the fact that you are aging. However, here are some averages of what can be expected as you reach certain age plateaus:

Age Forty

- At age forty, the body will burn 120 fewer calories a day than at age thirty, making weight harder to control.
- The body will become five-eighths of an inch shorter at age forty than at age thirty and will continue to shrink by about

one-sixteenths of an inch a year because of changes in posture, bone loss, and compression of the spongy disks that separate the vertebrae.

- Changes in the inner ear may erode the ability to hear higher frequencies for men, who lose hearing more than twice as fast as women do.
- The eyes will begin to have trouble focusing on close objects as your lenses become thicker.

Age Fifty

- Female Boomers will experience menopause, fertility will end, and lower estrogen will speed bone loss and raise the risk of heart disease.
- The eye's sensitivity to contrast will decline and the ability to see in dim light or under conditions of glare, or to catch sight of moving objects, will diminish.
- The loss of strength becomes measurable as muscle mass diminishes.
- Your vulnerability to infections and cancer will increase: the thymus, a gland that plays the key role in the immune system, will shrink by 85–90 percent.

Age Sixty

- It will become more difficult to carry on a conversation, especially in large groups and especially for men, as high-frequency hearing deteriorates further.
- Your pancreas, which processes glucose, will work less efficiently. Blood-sugar levels will rise and more Baby Boomers will be diagnosed with adult-onset diabetes.
- Joints will become stiff in the morning, particularly the knees, hips, and spine, because of wear and tear on the cartilage that cushions them.
- Your sexual desires and performance may begin to diminish, but with the introduction of Viagra many common sexual dysfunctions will improve or no longer exist.

Age Seventy

When you reach the age of seventy, you may expect the following:

- Your blood pressure will be 20–25 percent higher than it was in your twenties because your thicker, stiffer artery walls can't flex as much with each heartbeat.
- Your reaction to loud noises and other stimuli will be delayed as your brain's ability to send messages to the extremities will slow.
- Your short-term memory will decline with changes in brain function.
- More than half of men will show signs of coronary-artery disease.
- Your sweat glands will shrink or stop working (this is true for both men and women) and the risk of heatstroke will increase.

Age Eighty

- Women, in particular, will become more susceptible to falling and to disabling hip fractures due to a loss of over half the bone mass in their hips and upper legs.
- Almost half of those over the age of eighty-five will show signs of Alzheimer's disease.
- At maximum exertion, the heart will beat about 25 percent slower than it did at age twenty, but it will tend to compensate by expanding and pumping more blood per beat.
- Your personality will not change significantly as you age. If you were optimistic and good humored at the age of thirty or forty, chances are excellent that you will remain so most of your life. In other words, a cranky eighty-year-old was probably a cranky thirty-year-old.

Individual Differences in Physical Health

As we examine the overall statistics about the aging and health of middle-aged Baby Boomers, we are reporting generalities that do not cover many specific variations. For example, those with more education and income report better health, and have lower mortality rates, than those less well off. Race and the socioeconomic factors associated with it are also relevant. For example, the death rate for middle-aged African-Americans is twice that of whites. Gender can be an important factor as well. Men are much more likely to suffer fatal illnesses such as heart disease, while women are more likely to suffer chronic disabilities such as arthritis. The overall death rate for middle-aged men is three times that of women. Differences between the health of one individual and another are also affected by genes and by social factors that correlate with education, income, and race.

The Female Biological Clock

Between the late forties and early fifties, the female Baby Boomer can expect to reach her menopause as ovulation and menstruation stop. The term "change of life" refers to the time, lasting about three years, during which the woman's body adjusts to the production of much lower levels of the hormone estrogen.

The most obvious symptoms experienced during menopause are hot flashes, hot flushes, and cold sweats. These symptoms are all caused by a temporary disruption in the body mechanisms that constrict or dilate the blood vessels to maintain body temperature. The lower estrogen levels produce many other changes in the female body including drier skin, less vaginal lubrication during sexual arousal, loss of some breast tissue, more brittle bones, and an increased risk of heart attack.

Low doses of estrogen may be recommended for female Baby Boomers who are at risk for osteoporosis, the condition of thin and brittle bones that leads to increased fractures and frailty in old age. A diet high in calcium lessens the likelihood of developing osteoporosis. It has been recommended that you consume at least 1,200 milligrams of calcium per day, either through the foods you eat or by taking a calcium supplement.

The Male Sociological Clock

When the male Baby Boomer reaches middle age, he will not notice any sudden downward shift in reproductive ability or hormonal levels. There is no physiological "male menopause," and most men will continue to produce sperm indefinitely. Although there are important age-related declines in the number and motility of sperm, men are theoretically able to father a child in late adulthood. Similarly, the average levels of testosterone will decline gradually with age.

With only a few exceptions, the biological clock of females necessitates that they have their children by the time they reach their forties. This unavoidable fact may explain why many women begin to feel an urgency for commitment in their twenties and thirties. With men, however, it has always been a different story.

In the past many men have felt that they could wait until they were good and ready to father children and that they could still select from a highly desirable dating pool of smart and attractive young women. Based on recent research involving one thousand women between the ages of twenty-one and thirty, 71% of whom have attended college, men should not make such assumptions! According to the responses in the survey, many women feel that the male's *sociological* clock is ticking.

When the young women in the survey were asked how large an age gap is acceptable when they date someone, only 11% would venture an age gap above ten years. When they were asked why women would date men over forty, the most popular answer was money. Another 34% said older men were more emotionally stable, and 14% cited the search for a father figure. Only 2% listed looks as the reason. When the one thousand participants in the survey were asked at what age men are the most attractive, 41% identified the late twenties, 9% felt attracted to men older than thirty-five, and only 3% mentioned men over the age of forty. When asked at what age men are good in bed, only 6% said they preferred men over thirty-five as a sex partner.

Although the biological clock places pressure on women to settle down, if the results of this survey are valid, it is the sociological clock that does the same for men. It is less concrete and easier to break, but it exists.

Of course, there are individual differences, and these findings may not apply to you, especially if you are rich and/or famous. There's an old saying that there's always going to be fish in the sea, but as the male Baby Boomer gets older, his net will become much smaller and the fish a lot scarcer.

Heart Disease and Cancer—The Leading Killers of Aging Baby Boomers

The relationship between the aging Baby Boomer and disease is a complex one. Aging and disease are not synonymous: it is natural that a person's body will gradually weaken overall with age; it is not natural that the person will develop any particular disease. Most Baby Boomers probably consider their health good or excellent and on physical examinations are found to be quite well. Whether a particular person is seriously ill or in fine health depends not on age, but on genetic factors, past and current lifestyle (including eating and exercise habits), and psychological factors such as social support and a sense of control over one's daily life.

According to medical data, normal aging reduces the functioning of the heart, especially in times of exercise and stress. Normal aging also reduces the elasticity of the cardiovascular system. However, aging in itself does not cause heart disease. Many older Baby Boomers may show a number of risk factors related to heart disease such as elevated blood pressure, a high cholesterol level, obesity, lack of exercise, and a history of smoking. Over time, the interaction of these accumulating risk factors with the general weakening of the heart and relevant genetic weaknesses make the aging Boomer increasingly vulnerable. Research data reveal that heart attacks cause about 40% of all deaths over age sixty-five.

A relationship also exists between aging and cancer, the cause of about 20% of all deaths in the elderly. Some of the factors that may lead to cancer include genetic vulnerability and environmental risks such as exposure to asbestos or tobacco smoke. As people age, the potential for cancer is more likely to become manifest, and cure is more difficult.

The immune system provides the body with the ability to defend itself against outside invaders such as viruses and insiders such as cancer cells. The immune system works by destroying abnormal substances in the circulatory system, mainly with two types of "attack" cells. B-cells (manufactured in the bone marrow) create antibodies that attack specific invading bacteria and viruses. T-cells (manufactured by the thymus gland) produce specific substances that attack infected cells of the body. T-cells and B-cells produce efficient antibodies and strengthen the immune system.

With age there is a reduction in the power of both T-cells and B-cells, as well as in the efficiency of the mechanisms that regulate them. These changes help explain why most forms of cancer become much more common with age and why certain other illnesses, including some strains of the flu, are much more serious in an adult than in a child.

Causes of the Aging Process

Wear and Tear Theory—The oldest, most general theory of aging is the wear and tear theory, which compares the human body to a machine. Just as the parts of an automobile begin to give out as mileage adds up, so the parts of the human body deteriorate with each year of use, as well as with accumulated exposure to pollution, radiation, inadequate nutrition, disease, and various other stresses. According to this theory, we wear our bodies out just by living our lives.

It seems clear that the notion of wear and tear applies to some diseases and problems in some organs and body parts, but it is not very helpful in explaining the aging process overall.

Cellular Theory—The cellular theory of aging suggests that aging is the result of the accumulation of accidents that occur during cell reproduction.

Free Radicals Theory—This theory of aging began with the observation that some of the body's metabolic processes can cause electrons to separate from their atoms, resulting in atoms with unpaired electrons. These atoms, called free radicals, are highly unstable and capable of reacting violently with other molecules in the cell, sometimes splitting them or tearing them apart. The most critical damage caused by free radicals occurs in DNA molecules, producing errors in cell maintenance and repair that over time may eventually contribute to such diseases as cancer, diabetes, and arteriosclerosis. Free radicals damage cells, affect organs, and accelerate diseases. The gradual accumulation of damage as the individual ages may be one of the causes of the aging process.

Error Catastrophe Theory—When the systems of the body, especially the immune system, are in shape, the effects of cellular damage are minor, held in check by other cells that destroy seriously damaged cells and take over the work that imperfect cells no longer perform. As the immune system declines and the processes of repair and healing become less efficient, the number of errors can become so extensive that the body can no longer control or isolate the errors, leading to what has been called an error catastrophe. At this point the normal, healthy aging process gives way, disease overtakes the person, and death occurs.

Cross-Linkage Theory—The theory of cellular aging focuses on cross-linkage, the biochemical process through which certain kinds of molecules become linked with other kinds. With time, certain proteins of the body, notably collagen and elastin, which form the connective tissue that bind the cells of the body together, become cross-linked to other protein molecules. As this cross-linkage occurs, the proteins become less elastic and more brittle. For example, the skin becomes less elastic, more wrinkled, and feels dry and leathery with old age, precisely because more of its collagen is cross-linked. Cross-linkage may also be the underlying cause of major changes in the cardiovascular system, such as hardening of the arteries. In fact, increasing cross-linkage may be synonymous with aging, making each cell of the body less efficient.

Programmed Senescence Theory—Some scientists contend that, just as we are genetically programmed to reach various levels of biological maturation at fixed times, we are genetically programmed to die after a fixed number of years.

The Genetic Clock Theory—According to one theory, the DNA that directs the activity of every cell in the body also regulates the aging process. Our genetic makeup acts, in effect, as a genetic clock, triggering hormonal changes in the brain and regulating the cellular reproduction and repair process. As the genetic clock gradually "switches off" the genes that promote growth, there is speculation that genes that promote aging are switched on. The damage associated with aging continues to accumulate until one or more body systems can no longer function, and a natural death occurs. The fact that aging and death seem to be genetically programmed does not mean that we can predict when an individual will die naturally.

Living Longer

Three remote areas of the world—one in the former Soviet Union, one in Pakistan, and one in Peru—have become famous for having large numbers of people who enjoy unusual longevity. In these places, late adulthood is not only long but is also usually quite vigorous.

In the United States, a number of studies have examined the characteristics of individuals who have lived for 100 years or more. One such study is the Baltimore Longitudinal Study of Aging. Its basic purpose is to determine how different body organs change over time.

Some research has found that as Baby Boomers reach fifty years of age, they become suddenly serious about living to 100, and would like to get there in reasonably good health. There is a fear of losing independence and the ability to fend for oneself. A growing body of research suggests that chronic illness is not an inevitable consequence of aging, but more often the result of lifestyle choices. However, there are a number of things you can do to lengthen your life.

People 100 years old or older are the fastest growing segment of the American population. There are now 61,000 people in the United States who are more than 100 years old. It is estimated that by 2020 there will be 214,000. The Census Bureau projects that one in nine Baby Boomers born between 1946 and 1964 will survive into their late nineties and that one in 26 (about 3 million total) will reach the age of 100. A century ago the odds of living that long were about one in 500. (Berger, 1988)

Since 1980, the disability rate has fallen steadily among people who are sixty-five and older. Medical research has found that the oldest of the old often enjoy better health than people in their seventies. In a 1995 study, the Health Care Financing Administration calculated that medical expenditures for the last two years of life—statistically the most expensive—averaged $22,600 for people who die at age seventy, but just $8,300 for those who make it past 100.

Physical and Psychological Characteristics of Centenarians

In general, centenarians share the following characteristics:

- They possess superior intelligence, a keen interest in current events, and a good memory.
- They enjoy freedom from anxiety and few illnesses.
- They are not prone to worry.
- Many require fewer medications.

- They had independence of choice in their vocations. While employed, they tended to be their own bosses, and the majority did not retire early.
- They enjoy life, feel optimistic, and have a marked sense of humor.
- They are easily adaptable and prefer living in the present with its many changes.
- They are not preoccupied with death.
- They are religious in the broad sense, but they are not religious fanatics.
- They are moderate eaters. Their diet includes a variety of foods high in protein and low in fat.
- Most drink coffee.
- They have no uniformity with regard to the consumption of alcoholic beverages.
- Some abstained from smoking, but a few smoked very moderately when they were younger.

Socrates once said, "There is only one good, knowledge, and one evil, ignorance." This statement should guide us in all of our actions, especially where our health is concerned. Many of us do not have the correct idea of how to maintain good physical or mental health. When illness strikes, we rely on doctors to cure us. Nature has provided us with a wonderful immune system, and we must take proper care of this inner healing force.

Our modern lifestyles have gotten us off the right track, with fast foods, alcohol abuse, drug dependencies, a polluted environment, and high-tech stress. Nature intended to fuel our inner healing force with the right natural substances to enable the body to function up to its fullest potential. Nature's resources—whole foods, vitamins and minerals, enzymes, amino acids, etc.—are designed for use in our immune systems. Because many of us lack even the basic knowledge as to what our bodies need to function properly, we allow ourselves to get out of balance and become susceptible to all sorts of illnesses.

Baby Boomers, no less than any other persons, should take an active part in maintenance of their health and in the treatment of their disorders with the guidance of a health care professional. The more you learn about nutrition and complimentary medicine, the better prepared you will be to take the active role in prevention. Attitude is also an important factor in maintaining health and in healing. You must have a positive state of mind in order to bring harmony to the body. The body (lifestyle), spirit (desire), and mind (belief) must come together if you are to have better health.

The past decade has brought to light much new knowledge about nutrition and its effects on the body and the role it plays in disease. By understanding the principles of holistic nutrition, you can improve the state of your health, stave off disease, and maintain a harmonious balance in your body.

BABY BOOMER STRATEGY PLANNER

1. BRAINSTORMING

2. OBJECTIVE - TOP PRIORITY GOAL

Definition:

SPECIFIC DESCRIPTION

3. PRIMARY BARRIERS

1.

2.

3.

4. MOST APPARENT STRATEGY

ALTERNATE STRATEGY I

ALTERNATE STRATEGY II

5. INITIATION DATE

PROCEDURE HURDLING BARRIERS

MOST APPARENT STRATEGY

ALTERNATE STRATEGY I

ALTERNATE STRATEGY II

6. COMPLETION DATE

7. REWARDS

Chapter 9

Becoming Physically Fit

"Becoming physically fit requires an entirely new mind-set so that you can begin to develop eating patterns that you can live with for the rest of your life."

To function well, excellent physical health isn't an option—it's an absolute necessity. If you have a sound and fit body, every aspect of your life will be enhanced and you will approach all of your activities with more energy and enthusiasm. If you aren't physically fit, you may end up going through your golden years like a sluggish sloth, and your life itself may be threatened. Many of these threats are self-inflicted through overindulgence in food or alcohol; consumption of tobacco products; or exhaustion from overwork, too much worry, and too little rest.

To achieve optimum physical health, regular exercise and a well-balanced diet are essential. This is a fact that is stated time and time again, yet too few Americans today take it seriously enough. If you want to live to a *healthy* old age, you have to take action and control of your health *before* your body begins to deteriorate beyond repair.

Controlling the Human Clock—Rethinking Our Ideas about Old Age and Longevity

As we approach the end of the twentieth century, the average life expectancy for a White American is seventy-six years and for an African-American it is seventy-one years. However, as we all know, millions of people of both races live decades longer. All across America and throughout the industrialized world, people are living to ripe old ages undreamed of just a few decades ago. For example, there are over 60,000 centenarians in America alone. (Berger, 1988)

There are many factors that account for longevity. Genes have a lot to do with it, of course, especially those genes that help people resist such major diseases as cancer, stroke, and other age-related illnesses. Now, for the first time in the history of humankind, we are coming to recognize and understand that each one of us can have a say-so, to some extent, in the number of years we will live, rather than leaving the matter purely to chance. To achieve longevity, good health habits matter a great deal, especially when we consider that seven of the ten leading causes of death in the United States are from diseases related to lifestyle. Cancers due to smoking and improper diet, and high blood pressure and diabetes due to obesity are only a few examples. Although germs are an important factor in disease, our susceptibility to germs is related to our overall health.

In addition to good health habits, other elements important to longevity include self-confidence, an independent spirit, a positive mental attitude, a sense of humor, a stable disposition, and a persevering nature. Last, but not least, religion seems to play an important role in the lives of many of the healthy and happy centenarians.

In terms of quality of life, what can a Baby Boomer expect if he or she lives to the age of ninety or 100? And what is the point of striving to live to a ripe old age if you are going to end up ill, incapacitated, or financially destitute? In other words, is longevity a worthy goal to aim for? If you believe it is, then how do you begin to plan for it—physically, psychologically, and financially? What must you do now to get ready to enjoy the last few decades of your life? Let's take a closer look at the role physical fitness will play in determining whether your "golden years" are really golden.

Nutrition and Weight Management—Why Getting Older Doesn't Have to Mean Getting Fatter

One of the most important keys to achieving good health and a high energy level is staying fit. Keeping your weight under control seems to be a prerequisite for living to a ripe old age. It is very amusing sometimes to listen to centenarians talk about their lifelong eating and drinking habits (you have to wonder sometimes how much is truth and how much is exaggeration) when they are interviewed on TV or radio and are asked to speculate on what contributed to their longevity. Think about it for a moment—no matter what witty comments the centenarians might make about their lifestyles and the foods they enjoy, are any of them overweight? Have you ever seen a fat 100-year-old? Probably not, because the obese individuals have long since died, perhaps as much as fifteen or twenty years ago, while their trim and fit companions and friends are still kicking and enjoying life.

Today, more Americans are obese (children as well as adults) than at any other time in our country's history. During the past two or three decades, large segments of the adult population in many other countries have become obese as well, partly due to the ready availability of American-type fast foods and processed foods. Maturing Baby Boomers, especially, are finding it increasingly difficult to maintain a healthy weight and to stay in shape. Federal statistics indicate that 42% of women and 35% of men ages forty-five to fifty-five weigh at least 20% more than their desirable weight. (Berger, 1988)

It has been determined that the average man or woman will gain at least one pound a year between the ages of twenty-five and fifty-five, while at the same time losing a half pound of muscle per year. Small wonder then that with increasing age comes increasing girth and flab! Another astonishing fact that many people aren't aware of is that an individual can easily gain ten pounds per year merely by eating an extra 100 calories per day. Whether those extra calories enter the body in the form of a fat-free cookie or a piece of fruit, those few extra daily calories will add on the extra pounds over the course of time unless you work them off through exercise or some other physical activity.

You may recall that the old height-weight charts issued by the Metropolitan Life Insurance Company listed desirable weights according to a person's age and gender. For example, those Met Life charts indicated that it was acceptable for a fifty-year-old female of average height to weigh some twenty pounds more than a twenty-five-year-old woman of the same height. Men were also allowed to gain weight as they aged, but to a lesser extent.

In 1995, new federal guidelines were issued that don't allow for *any* weight gain as you age. However, in studies conducted by the

National Institute on Aging, it has been determined that "adults who fatten up a bit as they age live longer than those who lose weight" (*Newsweek,* April 21, 1997, p. 60).

It's no great secret why people of any age gain weight. They consume more calories than they burn, and the excess turns into fat—3,500 extra calories put *into* your body translates into an extra pound of fat *onto* your body. Why do people have a tendency to gain weight as they grow older?

- As people age, they become less active physically and lead a more sedentary lifestyle.
- To a large extent, they continue to eat the same ample portions of food that they ate when they were younger and more active.
- They don't exercise enough to maintain their muscle strength.

Even though a large percentage of the population has been on a diet at least once in their lives, most people have only a vague comprehension of how many calories they consume each day. Part of this is because they don't pay attention to how much they eat as they nibble or "graze" throughout the day or when they sit down for a full meal. At breakfast they may read the newspaper while chewing on a large crusty bagel slathered with cream cheese, or they may chomp down on a fat-free muffin that contains more than 500 calories. While eating lunch they may be involved in an animated conversation with friends or colleagues and then, suddenly, they are surprised to see that their plate is empty, even though they have no conscious awareness of consuming the food that was on it. At dinner, they will consume a couple thousand calories while watching TV, and they will hardly taste what they are eating because they are so engrossed in the program.

Over the past twenty or thirty years, there have been literally scores of diets that have become faddish and popular (partly through heavy advertising by their promoters). Some of them are actually dangerous to a person's health if followed for an extended period of time. Millions of individuals who have been overweight for much of their adult lives have gone on and off these fad diets without achieving any positive results. If dieting isn't the answer—as it has proven time and again not to be—what is? Losing weight sensibly and keeping it off permanently involves four important steps:

- Changing your eating habits
- Changing your attitudes about food
- Changing your lifestyle
- Getting more exercise

Changing Your Eating Habits—Easier Said Than Done?

Basically, eating healthier means eating more nutritious foods, including more fruits and vegetables, and eliminating or cutting down on junk food, sweets, and saturated fats. There is still a lot of controversy about how often a person should eat and how much food should be consumed at any one time. Some nutritionists and other experts on weight control suggest that the best way to lose weight or maintain your desirable weight is to eat four or five small meals evenly spaced throughout the day rather than consuming the usual three large meals of breakfast, lunch, and dinner. Other experts recommend only two full meals a day (breakfast and lunch or breakfast and dinner) plus several small snacks of fruit, yogurt, salad, etc.

Contrary to what many people believe, the time of day that you eat seems to be important also. Experiments have found that if you eat the largest portion of your food (up to 80%) before two o'clock in the afternoon, you will lose more weight and do a better job of maintaining your weight than if you eat most of it during the late afternoon or evening hours. Apparently, your metabolism works at a faster pace during the early part of the day (probably because you are more active then), and you will therefore burn the calories as quickly as you consume them.

Regardless of how often you eat, it is essential that you eat a variety of foods from the well-known United States Department of Agriculture (USDA) Food Guide Pyramid. Very few adults eat enough vegetables, for example, especially the green, leafy variety, which are rich in vitamins and low in calories. Be sure to supplement your diet daily with vitamins and minerals. It is also important to include an adequate amount of calcium and protein in your diet. Loss of bone density can cause osteoporosis, and loss of muscle tissue will make you flabby and weak. These are two problems that can play havoc with your health and physical well-being as you get older, unless you start to take preventive measures now.

There are a number of practical ways to begin to take control of your eating habits.

- Keep a food diary (see Exercise 9.1 at the end of this chapter for instructions on how to keep your own personal food diary) to determine your personal eating patterns and to assess the quantity of food you eat in a typical day.
- Get into the habit of eating smaller portions at every meal.
- Eliminate most desserts and sweets and nonnutritional junk food.
- Beware of some of the fat-free foods, especially if you have a tendency to confuse "fat-free" with "calorie-free." Just because a food item is fat-free doesn't mean you won't get fat if you eat large quantities of it!
- At home, try to eat in the same place every day, so that you associate the pleasure of eating with a particular room or area in your home or apartment. If you enjoy watching TV while you eat, try to concentrate more on the food than on the TV program. Eat slowly and savor the food's aroma, texture, and taste.
- Drink plenty of water, at least sixty to seventy ounces per day. Most Americans are chronically dehydrated simply because they don't drink enough water. Not only does water eliminate waste from burned-up fat, but it will also help prevent you from looking like a dried-up prune. A noted nutritionist has written about how people will spend $60 for a jar of fancy moisturizing cream when what they really should do is drink more water. There may be other physical benefits from drinking water as well. Some doctors have theorized that a lot of chronic back pain, perhaps even rheumatoid pain, results from an insufficient amount of water in the system.
- If you are feeling ravenous just before a meal, eat a few crackers or a piece of fruit or munch on raw vegetables ten or fifteen min-

utes before your regular meal. This will take the edge off your hunger and you won't eat as fast or as much when you sit down for the full meal. Another strategy is to drink a large glass of water or fruit juice (tepid, not chilled) before a meal. Many people find that this gives them a full feeling, even if only momentarily, and helps them to eat less.

• If you are trying to lose weight, hide your scale in the closet. It is hazardous to your mental health to weigh yourself every day. Once a week or every ten days is quite enough. If you hop onto the scale once or twice a day, hoping and praying that you have lost a few more ounces, you will undoubtedly become discouraged if you don't lose for several days. Keep in mind that your weight may fluctuate frequently by several pounds from fluid retention or fluid loss, so it is better to stay off the scales for as long as you can hold out. Then, when you do weigh again, in all probability you will discover that you have lost more pounds than you had anticipated.

Changing Your Attitudes About Food

What we have described are the physical aspects of eating and losing weight, but the psychological components are equally as important. One reason it is so hard to lose weight by dieting is because the typical diet is so rigorous and so restrictive that it is almost impossible to "stay on it" and stay sane long enough for it to be effective. When you consider that most people regard dieting as a serious form of deprivation and punishment, it is no wonder that the dieter soon becomes so stressed out that he or she goes off the diet just to relieve the inner stress and anxiety. More likely than not, the unsuccessful dieter will experience a loss of self-esteem that may be more damaging in the long run than if the individual had never tried dieting and had maintained the heavier weight. So life becomes a vicious cycle of off-and-on dieting and yo-yo weight loss, and there are no long-term benefits from any of it.

Becoming physically fit requires an entirely new mind-set so that you can begin to develop eating patterns that you can live with for the rest of your life. Both your eating habits and your feelings about food need to be changed forever. There are several ways to begin this process:

- First of all, stop chastising yourself for the physical condition you are in. It's not the end of the world. You may be out of shape but you are still alive, still relatively healthy, and there is still time to do something about your fitness problem.
- Stop telling yourself that you are going on a long-term diet next week, next month, or next year. It's probably not going to happen. Dieting hasn't worked for you in the past, so why should it work for you in the future?
- Stop thinking and believing that you are worthless and weak in character because you can't stay on a low-calorie diet program. Blame the diet, not yourself. Near-starvation diets don't work. Nobody can stay healthy and energetic and maintain their emotional equilibrium on a few hundred calories a day.
- Eliminate the word "diet" and the phrase "going on a diet" from your vocabulary and your consciousness. D-I-E-T is a vicious four-letter word that has caused more anxiety and more distress to more people than perhaps any other single word in the English language!
- Start a sensible weight-control program that you can stick with for the rest of your life. Begin by eating healthier, more nutritious foods. Focus on becoming physically fit rather than on losing weight.
- Try to burn off several hundred calories each day by exercising rather than starving yourself.
- Practice visualizing yourself as a trim, slim, energetic, and fit person. Hold this mental picture in your mind as you fall asleep at night and soon you will probably start dreaming of yourself in this way. It is almost inevitable that you will wake up feeling happy and refreshed and marveling at how wonderful you looked and felt in your dream. If you will replay this mental image of your new healthy self every time you sit down to eat a meal or a snack, it will strengthen your resolve to eat less and to eat healthier as well.

Changing Your Lifestyle

- Don't eat because you are bored or because you are depressed and have nothing better to do. Don't allow food to become the most important thing in your life.
- Get involved, keep busy. Take a walk, visit a friend, go to a movie, or to a museum, do volunteer work—do anything but sit home and eat!

Getting More Exercise—How to Learn to Enjoy It

Next to the word *diet*, the average out-of-shape adult probably abhors the word *exercise* more than any other word in the English language—or any other language. All too often, the word exercise conjures up images of panting, sweating young bodies in tight, bright Spandex outfits going through all kinds of torturous gyrations on the gym floor or at the health club. We just know in our hearts that, even if we wanted to, we could never do those kinds of strenuous exercise routines. Our knees and our backs just couldn't take it.

What about all those huffing and puffing anthropoids with small hips, skinny legs, and little antennas sticking above their ears who jog around our neighborhoods with such glazed looks on their faces? We can't help but wonder—if exercising is so much fun, then why do they always look so out of it and so pained?

From these few simple illustrations, it is obvious that we need to change our imagery and our attitudes about exercise and understand more accurately what it is and what it is not. We have always been indoctrinated with the erroneous theory of "no pain, no gain." Nancy Clark, a noted sports nutritionist and author, has said that it is important to keep in mind that the E in the word exercise stands for enjoyment, not for excruciating pain.

In addition, we can't help but remember with chagrin all those times in our younger years when we spent a ton of money to join a health club and then dropped out after only one or two visits. Thus, we still view exercise as something painful or boring, or something we are going to start doing—someday.

This is an unfortunate attitude, because a regular program of exercise not only benefits a person's overall physical health, including the cardiovascular system, but his or her psychological and emotional health as well. Regular exercise reduces stress and anxiety, keeps your metabolism higher, boosts your self-esteem by giving you the feeling that you are in charge of your life, and causes you to pay more attention to your body's needs.

Consider how even the simplest exercise, such as a brisk walk around the block, can help get rid of the mental cobwebs and that sluggish "blue" feeling that comes upon us all from time to time. After such an outing, we return to our home or office feeling rejuvenated and ready to face the tasks before us. Another important benefit to exercise that most people aren't aware of is the pumping of highly oxygenated blood through the brain, which is believed to increase a person's intelligence and creativity.

So how can maturing Baby Boomers develop a sensible exercise program that they can stick with? And what can kind of exercise is best?

Aerobics has long been touted as just about the best form of exercise because it gives the cardiovascular system such a good workout. Unfortunately, it is the bouncing around, jumping up and down version of aerobics that we think of first when we hear the term. Aerobics actually means any form of physical conditioning that improves your respiratory and circulatory functions and gets your heart rate up to a certain level and keeps it there for at least twenty minutes. In addition to jogging or performing a series of exercises at a gym or at home, aerobics also includes swimming, cycling, climbing stairs, and walking—activities that can be performed without too much difficulty by even the most sedentary Baby Boomer.

People who have acquired the attitude that they "hate to exercise" have a very limited and narrow view of what exercise consists of, and all too often they think that gym-type aerobics is the only exercise that is beneficial. They seem to forget the fact that there are many pleasant ways to exercise. Since listing them all would take pages, we will mention only a few of the more pleasurable and popular forms of exercise here—playing golf, tennis, handball, softball, shooting baskets with your children or grandchildren, gardening, cycling, hiking, climbing a mountain—the list goes on and on.

It is important to determine which exercises are best for you personally and, depending on your stamina and agility, whether you want to exercise alone or with a friend. The following tips and suggestions will assist you in developing your own personalized exercise program.

- Keep your formal exercise routine short and simple so that you won't tire of it and quit. Exercising for only twenty to thirty minutes a day is better than not exercising at all. According to Jane Fonda, who should certainly know, it isn't necessary to spend hours a day working out in order to stay in shape. In other words, you don't have to exercise until you drop.
- Make your exercise routine as convenient as possible. If you know you don't have the time or inclination to trek to a health club several times a week, then buy your own equipment and set up a simple fitness area in your home or apartment. If you already own a treadmill or a stationary bike, dust it off and move it to a prominent place such as the family room, master bedroom, or sun porch—anyplace where you can always see it and can hop on and off it frequently. If you don't have to go to an isolated area of your home to exercise, chances are you will do it much more often. If you don't already own personal exercise equipment, consider purchasing one of the multi-purpose machines that will strengthen your upper body and torso as well as your legs and hips.
- Make your exercise routine as pleasant as possible by doing other things while you exercise. Listen to music or audiobooks or watch TV.
- Walk, walk, walk. One of the primary reasons that maturing Baby Boomers are out of shape is because they have gotten into the habit of jumping into their cars for even the shortest trips. Try to get into the habit of walking a couple of miles several times a week, and try to walk as fast as you can. Although strolling along, chatting with your neighbors, looking at the flowers and watching the squirrels cavort may benefit you psychologically, to benefit physically you need to accelerate your heart rate and work up a little sweat by walking fast. If you can't walk outside because of inclement weather, consider doing it at a mall. In recent years "walking at the mall" has become a bit of a fad among seniors, but

you certainly don't have to be a certain age to participate in this pleasant activity. Just don't get too distracted by the shops or by other people.

• Try lifting weights. Unless you become addicted to this form of exercise, you won't do it enough to become muscle bound and lifting weights two or three times a week will help you preserve and rebuild muscle mass. This is another highly beneficial exercise that doesn't require expensive equipment or a trip to the gym.

• Try yoga instead of exercise. This is the approach taken by actress Dixie Carter who says she "can't stand exercise" but that yoga is a different matter. She adds that after only twelve minutes of yoga in the morning, she is renewed and can make it through the day. Jane Fonda also recommends yoga more than anything else.

Regularity is the key to success. Don't skip just because you are tired or sluggish or you don't have time. Make time. Find time. The most important thing is to get in the habit of exercising on a regular basis. Just twenty to thirty minutes a day is the minimum time that is needed.

EXERCISE 9.1—Keeping a Food Diary

Note: This is a worthwhile exercise even if you don't need to lose weight, because so many people, even those who consider themselves fit, don't always eat as healthily as they think they do.

Keep a written record of everything you eat for at least seven days. Most people don't realize how *much* they eat during a typical day or how many times they nibble while working at their desks at the office or watching TV at home. Writing down everything you eat for a week will give you a clearer picture of your daily food intake. Don't try to change your eating habits during this period because the purpose of this exercise is to determine how much you eat normally—and where and when.

Be diligent about jotting down what you eat as soon as you eat it, so you won't forget. We repeat: *write everything down*, even if it's only "a couple of bites" of this or that. A few nibbles and a few small snacks here and there throughout the day can add up to several hundred calories by the end of the day. However, we are not going to ask you to try to estimate your caloric intake for each day. That is probably impossible, especially if you are unfamiliar with calorie counting. More importantly, you need to get into the mind-set of eating healthy, rather than counting calories. One reason so many people are unable to stay on a diet is because of the onerous burden of having to eat the same number of calories every day and of having to measure and weigh every bite or ounce of food they eat.

In your food diary, list the portion size (large, medium, or small), the time of day, where you ate (at home, your office, at your desk or computer, at the kitchen table, in front of the TV, etc.), and what activities, if any, you were engaged in while eating.

All of this will give you a much clearer picture of your eating patterns. For example:

- When you eat, do you focus on your meal or snack or is your attention divided by work, television, conversation, etc.?
- Do you usually have a snack about the same time every morning or during the afternoon? Perhaps your blood sugar drops at this time and you need to eat something to become alert again. Or perhaps you snack just to have a momentary diversion in your routine.
- Do you always eat something before going to bed at night. If you do, ask yourself why? Are you really hungry then, or does eating late help you to relax and fall asleep faster? Is eating before bedtime simply a habit you've gotten into over the years?

These are examples of some of the questions that you will be able to answer after you have recorded and analyzed your eating patterns over a one-week period. You can perform this exercise for a longer period if you wish, especially if your eating habits change substantially from week to week.

After you have analyzed and summarized your food diary, be sure and hold onto it for awhile. A few months from now when you have substantially altered your eating habits, you will be amazed to see just how much food you used to eat, how often you ate it, and how unhealthy most of it was. Your reaction may be along the lines of "Good heavens, did I put *that* much junk food into my body *every* day!"

BABY BOOMER STRATEGY PLANNER

1. BRAINSTORMING

2. OBJECTIVE - TOP PRIORITY GOAL

Definition:

SPECIFIC DESCRIPTION

3. PRIMARY BARRIERS

1.

2.

3.

4. MOST APPARENT STRATEGY

ALTERNATE STRATEGY I

ALTERNATE STRATEGY II

5. INITIATION DATE

PROCEDURE HURDLING BARRIERS

MOST APPARENT STRATEGY

ALTERNATE STRATEGY I

ALTERNATE STRATEGY II

6. COMPLETION DATE

7. REWARDS

Chapter 10

Survival Strategies
For Successful Physical Health

Our bodies have a wonderful immune system that protects us from illness, and if we already have a physical problem, the immune system heals us.

D o you realize that to a large extent you are responsible for your own health? The task of your medical doctor is to help your body do what it can do so well on its own. Our bodies are great chemical factories. They produce our own natural tranquilizers and pain-killing chemicals called endorphins. An endorphin is a morphine-like substance that is said to be two hundred times more powerful than morphine. Our bodies have a wonderful immune system that protects us from illness, and if we already have a physical problem, the immune system heals us.

Many people don't make proper use of the immune system; instead they are causing or making physical problems worse. Although we take various medications for our illnesses, when we heal and get better it is often the result of an improved immune system.

We have already identified several factors that can predict successful aging. They include regular physical activity, proper nutrition, continued social connections, a feeling of well-being, and resiliency, which is the ability to bounce back after suffering a loss. Did you know that the best predictor of good health and long life is a person's level of education? In study after study, educational level is correlated with better health and with greater wealth. High levels of stress in addition to a lack of close friends or family can significantly reduce life expectancy. However, the governmental report entitled "Health, United States, 1998" found that each increase in income and education has a significant impact on health. The report also indicated that the death rate from heart disease declined 12% between 1990 and 1996. Death from cancer dropped by 5%, which stopped its steady climb for the first time.

Since Baby Boomers have identified cancer and heart disease as their two major health concerns, we will review the status of treatment for both of these prevalent and dreaded diseases.

Strategies for Cancer Treatment

The most commonly used treatments for cancer do not work; rather they seem to make the patient worse. Until the recent 5% drop in cancer deaths noted earlier, the death rates for the most serious cancers, such as those affecting the breasts, colon, prostrate, lung, uterus, and ovaries, have gone up despite the billions of dollars that have been spent in trying to find a cure.

The reason that there has not been any significant improvement in deaths from cancer is because the method of treatment is based on a faulty theory. Conventional cancer therapy purports that the body must be purged of cancer by toxic methods such as surgery, chemotherapy, and radiation therapy. We know from the deaths of over 500,000 people a year from cancer that conventional therapy doesn't work. Yet, the use of alternative therapies in this country is against the law. Therefore, cancer patients must submit to the toxic failure treatment available because there is no other choice.

At the beginning of this chapter, it was indicated that our illnesses are the result of a dysfunction of the immune system. Cancer represents a significant breakdown in our body's immune system. If a person is to survive cancer, the immune system must be strengthened so it can prevent the cancerous tumor from growing and it must eventually destroy the tumor. Therefore, the focus of our treatment should be on how to strengthen our immune system and our general health.

There are a number of ways the immune system can be strengthened, but most of the treatment methods for cancer are illegal in this country. One approach to cancer treatment using Immune Augmentative Therapy was started by Dr. Lawrence Burton in the mid-1960s at St. Vincent's Hospital in New York City. Dr. Burton isolated from blood four proteins that blocked the growth of cancer cells. On several occasions, he injected these proteins into cancerous mice and the cancer would disappear. Dr. Burton applied for an FDA Investigational New Drug permit for human cancer studies. He never received FDA approval, so he set up the Immunology Research Center in Freeport, Grand Bahamas Island. The center has successfully treated many cancer patients using Immune Augmentative Therapy. Although Dr. Burton died in 1993 from heart disease, the clinic continues to treat cancer patients under the direction of Dr. R. J. Clement and Dr. Donald Carrow.

In this country, Dr. Stanislow Burzynski in Houston, Texas, has isolated protein fragments from urine, which have been demonstrated in several studies to prevent cancer. It seems that these protein particles actually block the cancer chromosomes in your cells and facilitate the antitumor chromosomes. Dr. Burzynski has been under attack by the FDA. However, his work is receiving favorable support from other countries.

Preventing Cancer

The most important tactic for cancer is prevention. There is no form of prevention that is perfect, but there are ways in which you may reduce your risk of getting cancer. It has been estimated that up to 75 percent of cancer deaths could be prevented. Not only are the basics of cancer prevention simple, but they will also help reduce your risk of many other major diseases. (Whitaker, 1998)

Avoid Tobacco Exposure

Cigarette smoke causes 434,000 deaths a year in the United States due to heart disease, stroke, and emphysema. At least 144,000 lives are lost each year from smoking-induced lung cancer. An additional 2,000 to 4,000 deaths will occur each year from lung cancer brought on by exposure to other people's smoke. The carcinogens (cancer-causing substances) in smoke are absorbed into the blood, which carries them to other parts of the body where they do great harm. Many of these deaths could be prevented if people would stop smoking.

Limit Alcoholic Intake

A modest amount of alcohol doesn't increase a man's risk of cancer, although it may increase a woman's risk of breast cancer. Alcohol abuse can cause cirrhosis of the liver, which sometimes leads to liver cancer. It can also increase the risks of cancers of the mouth, throat, larynx, esophagus, and pancreas. Smokers who drink are at particularly high risk.

Eat Well

Since diet contributes to almost a third of cancer malignancies, nutrition is most important. By eating poorly, you increase your risk of cancer by exposing yourself to harmful substances and by depriving your body of protective nutrients.

The following is a dietary guideline for cancer prevention:

- Maintain a desirable body weight.
- Eat a variety of foods.
- Choose most of the foods you eat from plant sources, including minimally processed starchy foods.
- Eat five or more servings of fruits and vegetables a day.
- Eat high-fiber foods, such as whole grain products and legumes.
- Eat less fat, particularly from animal sources.
- Eat less meat and consume more dairy products, including low-fat milk and yogurts. If you eat red meat, limit yourself to 3 ounces a day.
- Limit your consumption of alcoholic beverages.
- Limit your consumption of nitrite-preserved, salt-cured, and smoked foods.

Use Supplements and Medications

It has been found that vitamin E supplements appear to reduce the risk of prostate cancer. Selenium has been associated with a substantial reduction in cancer of the prostrate, lung, colon, and rectum. Selenium appeared to reduce cancer deaths by 48 percent.

Another supplement that may help is aspirin. Low-dose aspirin has been proven to play a very important role in protecting patients with coronary artery disease from heart attacks and strokes, but be warned that aspirin can cause gastric irritation and bleeding.

Exercise Regularly

Exercise helps prevent cancer by burning calories, thereby fighting obesity. Exercise also speeds the elimination of waste products from the colon; thus, regular exercise substantially reduces the risk of colon cancer in both men and women. There is good evidence that exercise reduces the risk of breast and female reproductive tract cancers.

Avoid Sunlight

Ultraviolet radiation damages the DNA skin cells, causing potentially deadly malignant melanomas and other less serious skin cancers. Stay out of the sun, especially between 10 A.M. and 2 P.M., when the sun's rays are the strongest. Start protecting yourself now, and teach the rest of your family that there is no such thing as a healthy tan.

Avoid Infections

The human immunodeficiency virus (HIV) and various sexually transmitted viruses can cause cancer. Simple precautions that prevent the transmission of viruses through blood and body fluids should be nearly 100% effective.

Avoid Exposure to Radiation and Carcinogenic Chemicals

In large doses, medical X-rays can also increase the risk of cancer; get X-rays only when you really need them. Steer clear of asbestos fibers. Help clean up the environment from toxic pollutants in the air, water, and soil.

Lifestyle Change—The Best Medicine

Basic lifestyle changes can substantially reduce your risk of cancer; add early detection and top medical care, and you'll have a complete program. You'll also reduce your risk of high blood pressure, diabetes, obesity, osteoporosis, and other diseases.

Strategies to Prevent Heart Disease

The next major health problem that Baby Boomers can anticipate is heart disease. It is the number-one killer for both men and women. Heart disease is primarily a lifestyle disease. If you have heart disease and persist in an unhealthy lifestyle, it will only get worse as you get older. Once plaque gets into your arteries, it stays there forever unless you take steps to get it out. As the years go by, the plaque builds up in your blood vessels, narrowing the passage for blood flow, making your heart work harder and harder to get blood through your system. If things worsen, you may begin to suffer from angina, and eventually may have a heart attack.

One of the most powerful tools in treating heart disease is a low-fat diet. Study after study shows that a low-fat diet not only helps to prevent heart disease but actually reverses it. When the diet is combined with an effective exercise program, the benefits increase.

Nutritional supplements are also effective, as shown by two important Harvard studies. One six-year Harvard study of 21,000 doctors showed that those who took regular beta-carotene supplements had half as many strokes, heart attacks, and other heart problems as those who did not. In another Harvard study, nurses who took vitamin E had 36% less risk of heart attack than those who did not.

Vitamin E guards against heart disease by preventing low-density lipoprotein (LDL) or "bad" cholesterol from being oxidized by free radicals in your blood. A major study by the World Health Organization showed that a low level of vitamin E in the blood was twice as predictive of a heart attack than either high cholesterol levels or high blood pressure. Intake of 800 to 1,200 mg a day of vitamin E is recommended.

Vitamin C helps prevent damage to artery walls and helps to repair damaged artery walls. It is 95% effective in blocking cholesterol plaquing and elevates the level of high-density lipoprotein (HDL) or "good" cholesterol. Intake of 5,000 mg a day is recommended, divided into two or three doses.

Coenzyme Q-10 is an over-the-counter nutrient that can strengthen a weak heart. In one study published in the *American Journal of Cardiology*, 126 patients who took coenzyme Q-10 had an average survival rate that was years longer than expected. Intake of 150 mg a day is recommended for mild heart problems but up to 400 mg per day may be necessary for severe cases.

L-Carnitine is another over-the counter nutrient that can dramatically improve heart function in those with heart disease. It acts as a transporter of fat across cell membranes so that the fat can be burned as energy. Intake of 1,000 mg a day is recommended.

Fish oils are high in omega-3 fatty acids, which help improve your blood fat levels. They also help prevent blood clots, thus decreasing the risk of heart attacks and strokes. It is recommended that those with heart disease take five to ten capsules a day.

Cayenne pepper can help those with heart disease. Cayenne capsules can act as a general stimulant and reduce cholesterol build up. Gelatin capsules are best. Take three to four per day with food.

Magnesium can help control a skipping heart. Cardiac arrhythmia is one of the most frightening manifestations of heart disease. Given intravenously, it is a powerful stabilizer of heart rhythm. Take 500 to 1,000 mg a day as an oral supplement.

Controlling Your Cholesterol

An essential part of preventing heart disease is the reduction of your LDL, or bad, cholesterol levels while raising the HDL, or good, cholesterol levels. Much of what you do to control heart disease will also give you the cholesterol level you need. Consider the following:

- Increase your intake of dietary fiber.
- Take a daily supplement of garlic capsules.
- Take 400 mg of chromium picolinate per day.
- Take four doses of Gugu Plus #860 PSE per day. Gugu Plus contains gugulipid, a plant extract that has been shown to dramatically lower both blood cholesterol and triglycides.
- Take DHEA, which has been shown to be effective against heart disease in general.

Controlling Your Hypertension

High blood pressure can precipitate a sudden stroke or gradually destroy your heart, blood vessels, and kidneys. It is not a disease; it is a condition, and for most, it is the price we pay for living and eating the way we do. It becomes much more of a problem as we grow older, as obesity, smoking, and a high-fat diet gradually begin to take their toll.

In order to lower and control high blood pressure, it is recommended that you do the following:

Take medication. Ask your physician to prescribe a blood pressure medication to help lower your blood pressure.

Go on a low-fat diet. Fat elevates blood pressure by increasing the thickness of the blood and stimulating hormones that cause the blood vessels to constrict. Fat also increases weight, which usually raises blood pressure.

Increase your consumption of both potassium and magnesium. It is recommended that you take 1,000 mg per day of elemental magnesium. In addition, you should be eating two or three servings per day of fresh fruits and deep-green vegetables. To increase potassium, eat tangerines, oranges, bananas, dried peas, and beans. Magnesium/potassium aspartate (1,000 to 3,000 mg) is also recommended.

Take fish oils, which are high in omega-3 fatty acids. With omega-3 in your bloodstream, the blood flows more smoothly, with less resistance, and blood pressure falls.

Take garlic capsules.

Stop smoking. This can be a tough assignment for those who are addicted to nicotine, but you must stop smoking if you hope to lower your blood pressure.

Exercise. Develop a good exercise program of at least twenty minutes a day, three days a week. This helps lower your blood pressure by relaxing the muscles of your blood vessel walls and allowing them to expand, and by decreasing the thickness of your blood.

Strategies for Dealing with Prostate Gland Disorder

Approximately 75% of men over age fifty have measurable enlargement of the prostate gland, which can block the passage of urine from the bladder. Actually, an enlarged prostate is a natural result of growing older—the prostate begins a second growth spurt when you reach about age forty. Natural, however, doesn't always mean desirable. An enlarged prostate usually results in painful urination, even if the enlargement isn't cancerous. (Rosenfeld, 1998)

The most common treatment for this problem is surgery, in which part of the prostate gland is removed. About 400,000 of these procedures are done each year, but the results are far from satisfactory: Out of every 100 patients, an average of two die, eight have to be rehospitalized within three months for complications, five become impotent and twenty have to have the surgery repeated.

Other treatments include medications such as Proscar, and like most prescription drugs, it has undesirable side effects. There are much safer and more effective alternatives you can try to alleviate an enlarged prostate, which include the following:

Eat a low fat diet, including vegetables, rice, and grains. Include lots of zinc-rich foods in your diet.

Take a zinc picolinate supplement (30 to 60 mg) coupled with vitamin B-6 (50 mg).

Include the essential fatty acids. Take either a combination of three fish oil capsules or three evening primrose capsules per day.

Try a supplement containing the lipid extract of saw palmetto berries, which have been used for centuries to treat urinary problems. They are superior to the popular drug Proscar, without the side effects.

Microwave Treatment. There is a new microwave procedure that has been successfully used to reduce the size of an enlarged prostrate. Discuss this new treatment with your urologist.

Strategies for Dealing with Impotence

Impotence affects at least 30 million men, young and old, in this country. It is largely the result of various hormonal, vascular, and neurological causes and to a lesser extent, psychological factors. Many of these causes can now be treated.

Many men resort to testosterone supplements to improve their sexual functioning. Although testosterone production diminishes with age, there's usually enough to maintain libido and permit men, even in their eighties and older, to produce sperm and remain potent.

Many complex psychological and emotional factors can lead to impotence, but they account for only 20% of cases. The physical causes are related to medications, vascular disease, nerve, and other disorders.

Medications

Medications cause at least 25% of all cases of impotence. Drugs that lower blood pressure, antihistamines, painkillers, antidepressants, tranquilizers, phenylopropanolamine—all can result in impotence. If you're having a penetration problem, review every drug you're taking regardless of whether it's a prescription item, one you bought over the counter, or an herb.

Vascular Disease

Blood flowing into the penis is what makes an erection. The volume necessary to do so can be reduced not only by arteriosclerosis (hardening of the arteries) but also by physical injury. More than 100,000 men have been left impotent by damage to the penis from the seat of a bicycle or from the top tube of the bike's frame.

Nerves and Other Disorders

Anything that hurts the nerves carrying the messages from the brain to the penis can cause impotence. Some of the major culprits are: injury to the spinal cord or pelvis, accidental severance of the nerves during prostrate surgery, radiation, alcohol, and tobacco. Also, 50% of diabetic males have erectile dysfunction.

Treatment of impotence depends on its specific cause. Often this can be determined by a detailed personal and medical history as well as a thorough physical examination. The introduction of Viagra has had an enormous impact on the management of impotence. It also has changed society's attitude toward this condition. Viagra works by increasing the concentration in the penis of nitric acid, a dilator of blood vessels. The more nitric acid you have, the better the erection. The drug reduces the concentration of an enzyme that breaks down the nitric acid in the penis. Viagra comes in three different strengths—25, 50 and 100 milligrams—but the cost is the same for each, $8 to $10 per tablet. Men who have long-standing psychogenic impotence are the least likely to benefit from Viagra.

Other options to consider:

Vacuum Pumps

An acrylic cylinder is placed over the flaccid penis and attached to a pump. Squeezing the pump handle a few times creates a vacuum that draws air out of the cylinder and sucks blood into the penis, causing it to become erect.

Penile Injections

Several drugs, such as papaverine, phentolamine, and prostaglandin E, can produce an erection by relaxing the smooth muscle in the penis so that blood can flow into it. All of these drugs, however, have to be injected into the penis.

Penile Implants, Other Surgery and Treatment Approaches

If you have severe vascular disease or have suffered an injury to the interior of the penis, you will not respond to any of the procedures or drugs described previously. In that case, a surgeon can implant a device in the penis that will make it erect, reconstruct damaged arteries within the penis, or repair the varicose veins within it that are responsible for the "venous leak" (the rapid exit of the blood from that organ).

Promising Treatments on the Horizon

An oral preparation of phentolamine (Vasomax), now administered only by injection, is awaiting FDA approval and probably will be available soon. It takes fifteen to thirty minutes to work, and is expected to be effective in only 30% to 40% of cases.

A sublingual form of apomorphine that dissolves under the tongue and acts directly on the area of the brain that triggers erections may be marketed in a year or two. It is said to be 70% effective in men with psychologically caused impotence.

Strategies for Dealing with Arthritis

As you get older, your body wears down your joints with use. As the joint cartilage degenerates, it fragments and forms painful spurs. We often gain weight as the years creep by, giving our joints more to carry, and we often exercise less even although that's one of the best things we can do for arthritis. In females, arthritis is exacerbated by the history of wearing high-heeled shoes.

For arthritis, doctors generally prescribe aspirin or any of a number of other drugs, some of which can cause internal bleeding and block your body's ability to produce cartilage. This eventually leads to even worse arthritis, and the pain relief is often inadequate.

There are other approaches that can bring relief in many cases. The use of glucosamine sulfate (GS) helps your body produce healthy connective tissue at the joints, repairing damage that has already occurred and actually reversing arthritis. Barley juice, which is loaded with chlorophyll, is a potent anti-inflammatory agent. If you are under a physician's care for arthritis, discuss starting this approach as a therapeutic trial.

Here are some other approaches you will want to know about:

- *Eat a low-fat, mostly vegetable diet.* Some studies have shown that arthritis sufferers who are on all-vegetarian diets experience noticeable reduction in joint pain.
- *Take fish oils.* Fish oil decreases both arthritis inflammation and the accompanying pain. Ten capsules per day is recommended.
- *Take thymus gland supplements.*
- *Use pantothenic acid.* In a double-blind study, when two grams of pantothenic acid were given daily to arthritis patients, there was a significant reduction in the duration of morning stiffness and degree of disability as well as severity of pain.

Strategies for Dealing with Diabetes

Ninety percent of people who get diabetes have the adult-onset variety. This is partly because aging decreases our ability to handle sugars. But as we age, we usually gain weight and become sedentary, two of the greatest risk factors for diabetes. Insulin is the usual therapy, but is rarely necessary. Diet and nutrition are both cheaper and more effective. Follow this suggested routine:

First, remake your diet. Replace fat calories with complex carbohydrate calories. Fat tends to block the effect of insulin, while carbohydrates enhance it.

Second, get enough good exercise. Exercise enhances the effectiveness of insulin, and by itself can substantially reduce your need for medication. Exercise also stimulates weight loss when it is necessary.

Third, supplement your intake of vitamins and minerals. When you're diabetic, your body wastes enormous amounts of essential nutrients and vitamins—thus your requirement for these nutrients is markedly increased. In addition to antioxidants, it is recommended that you take vitamins B-6 (50 mg) and B-12 (40 mg) as well as the other B-complex nutrients. Also, supplement your diet with magnesium (1,000 mg) and chromium (400 mcg).

Strategies for Dealing with Digestive Problems

The main reason we have digestive problems is our diet. The problem becomes complicated for you after you reach age fifty. As you age, the motions that move the digested food through your intestines slow down, so food and waste stay in your system longer, allowing more water to be absorbed as the waste passes through your colon. The result is harder, drier stools. To make matters worse, your aging digestive system is less efficient at producing digestive enzymes for the stomach, liver, pancreas, and small intestine.

The answer to these problems is to give your digestive system more bulk in order to function properly. Fats, processed food, and sugars do not give you bulk, but fiber does. Fiber is not digested—it moves smoothly through the system, pushing other foods along with it. Without fiber, you get constipated.

Use this simple eating plan:

Step 1. Drink plenty of water every day—eight glasses or more. Among other things, it serves as a lubricant.

Step 2. Let complex carbohydrates be your staples. Complex carbohydrates are generally high in fibers and thus are very kind to your digestive tract. Include whole-grain foods (including bread and cereals), fresh vegetables, beans, and lentils.

Step 3. Snack on fresh, raw fruit, and vegetables; dried prunes, figs, and raisins; and popcorn (find the low-fat variety, and eat it without butter).

Step 4. If you are over fifty, consider taking supplements of hydrochloric acid and digestive enzymes to help your body digest your food better.

Strategies for Dealing with Fatigue or Low Energy

As you age, your metabolism slows down and becomes less efficient. If you need to charge up your energy reserves, start by checking the foods you eat. Your three meals a day may be your worst enemy. Sugars will give you a brief burst of energy, but will rob you of energy in the long term.

Here are some high-energy foods you can add to your diet:

pasta

brown rice and lentils

baked potatoes

cooked beans (such as in chili)

steamed or stir-fried vegetables with noodles

green salad with chicken breast and one or two slices of whole wheat bread

Of all the supplements to increase energy, potassium/ magnesium aspartate stands out as the most important. Both magnesium and potassium produce a sense of energy, and their effect is enhanced when they're combined in the aspartate salt form.

BABY BOOMER STRATEGY PLANNER

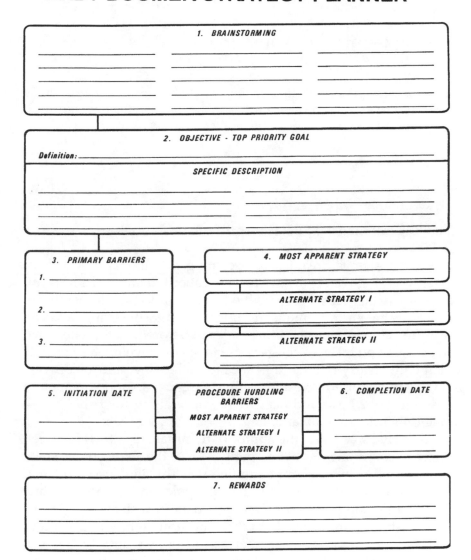

Chapter 11

Taking Control of Your Finances

"How you think and feel about money determines not only how much you have but also how much value it will have for you. . . . Redirect your thinking about money and the result will be a 'consciousness of prosperity.'"
—Earl Nightingale

The Key to Financial Success—Attitude or Action?

Have you always dreamed of becoming a millionaire or at least wealthy enough never to have to worry about finances again? If you are a maturing Baby Boomer who has begun to feel desperate because you haven't accumulated sufficient capital or savings and you want to achieve financial independence before it is too late, what steps have you taken to get started? Have you developed a concrete plan with clearly defined timelines for achieving your objectives? Have you begun to invest, or is investing just a vague dream and desire in your head and heart? Are you waiting for riches to fall magically into your lap and life?

You may have taken the appropriate initial steps toward developing a "consciousness of prosperity." Over the years you've spent a lot of time *thinking* about becoming wealthy and successful, and you've purchased a large number of books and manuals telling you how to motivate yourself and set goals, how to make a fortune in real estate or in the stock market, and how to buy and sell this, that, or the other. You have shelves of books whose titles begin *How To Get, How to Make, How to Be, How to Become.* You are well acquainted with *The Three Secrets . . . The Five Basic Steps . . . The Seven Habits . . . The Twelve Ingredients . . .* and *The Twenty Lessons . . .* You've ordered several of the expensive home-study courses advertised on the infomercials on late night cable TV, complete with audiocassettes and massive spiral notebooks; and you've also attended seminars on how to stop working for money and how to let money work for you.

When you bought the materials and attended the seminars, you had the best of intentions but once your initial enthusiasm wore off, how diligent were you in applying the principles and concepts suggested by the authors? Did you read only the first couple of chapters and listen to only one or two of the tapes before you became bored or distracted and put the materials aside to gather dust on a bookshelf?

It is true that each and every author of a get-rich-quick book claims to have found the magic elixir for achieving wealth and success. It is also true that often the only people who will ever became rich and successful from some of these books are the people who write, publish, and promote them. Did you ever stop to consider that perhaps the reason why you haven't benefited personally from the materials that you have spent a lifetime accumulating is because you failed to follow through—you never got around to practicing what the authors preached.

If there is any single theme that weaves in and out of the best of the motivational and success-oriented books, it is this—to become successful (personally as well as financially), you must have a focus, a sense of purpose, and a clear vision of where you want to go and what you hope to accomplish. In addition to vision, you must have a written plan, a sort of roadmap, for getting to your ultimate destination; but for some reason, you have never gotten beyond the thinking and dreaming stage.

Now, you're scared because your life is zooming by so fast. You feel frustrated and discouraged every time you learn that some of your colleagues and friends, who aren't any smarter or better educated than you and who haven't worked any harder over the years, are planning to retire in splendid luxury by the time they reach the age of 55. You shake your head in awe and ask yourself again and again

- How did *they* do it?
- How did they accumulate *that* much wealth?
- What did *I* do wrong—why haven't *I* done as well?
- Is it too late for me to get my financial act together now?

Some of the people who can afford to retire early may have had their own lucrative businesses that they sold or franchised, or they may have invested in real estate when the buying and selling of land and property was still a viable method of making a quick profit. But many of them held salaried positions, and they may never have had access to a large sum of money at any one time.

If an analysis could be made to determine the primary differences between you and "them"—between their savings and investing habits and yours—what would you learn? Chances are you would learn that for the past ten or twenty years while you were spending your income as soon as you received it, saving little and investing none at all, they were investing a portion of their earnings, *on a regular basis*, in stocks or mutual funds or some other long-term investment vehicle. With the rapid growth of some of these funds and through reinvestment of all dividends over the years, the small sums they invested regularly have now grown into an astonishingly large nest egg.

This situation is not remarkable or unusual. If you were to read the prospectuses of some of the major mutual funds, for example, you would see chart after chart indicating that for each $10,000 invested a mere ten or twelve years ago in certain growth funds and stocks, that money would have grown to $80,000 or $90,000 now.

The fact is, for whatever reason, you *didn't* invest $10,000—or any thousand. You deeply regret it, and you feel like kicking yourself every time you see the charts and statistics and you think of what might have been, but what can you do about it now? Is there any way you can ever catch up to ensure that you will have enough principal accumulated to retire in comfort, free from stress and worry?

The experts will tell you that it is never too late to get started on a savings and investment program. Even if you're a mature Baby Boomer, chances are good that you will live another thirty-five or forty years (or longer). You're vigorous and healthy and there's no reason why you can't continue to work well into your seventies—*if you want to,* and *if you love your work.* Besides, what's so great about being retired for thirty or forty years? We all know the stories of people who keeled over dead within a couple of years after retirement—perhaps from boredom! Seriously, instead of envying your neighbors and friends who are retiring early, give some thought as to what *you* want to do for the rest of your life. Surely you don't want to sit back with your feet up all of that time.

If you can't envision working in your same job or career for another decade or two, now might be the time to consider other alternatives. How many times have you thought about starting a business of your own someday, part-time or full-time. It is never too late to change careers, and it is never too late to take control of your life. It is a well-known fact that the people who love their jobs the most, the people who get the greatest pleasure from working, are usually those individuals who are their own boss or who have the most control over their working environment. Research also shows that the majority of the people who have made a great deal of money have made it doing something they love.

If you are short of ideas about new career or business choices, look around you to see how other people are making money (and having fun while doing it). The usual advice is to find a need and create a product or service to fill it, or start with an established product or service and find a way to improve on it. Spend a few hours reading some of the business and entrepreneurial magazines and you will discover that there are literally hundreds of business options that you might never have considered. You don't have to pay thousands of dollars to buy into a popular franchise (although for many people that may be the best way to go) but rather, read those business publications for ideas, and start something similar on your own.

Everyone knows that people who go into business for themselves must have courage, confidence, and enthusiasm. These are desirable traits for an investor also. As you begin your investment program, work on your attitudes and develop your own personal "prosperity consciousness." Whatever you decide to do with the rest of your life, at the very least do the following:

- **Believe in Yourself**—Dream big, think prosperous thoughts, and develop positive attitudes. Reassure yourself periodically that you have what it takes to succeed.
- **Define Your Goals and Write Them Down**—Work out a program of definite goals. Set up a schedule of deadlines. Focus on your

priorities. Realize that less important things can wait. Be specific about what you want to achieve and when. Write down your goals to clarify your thoughts. Goals that exist only in the mind will probably never be achieved.

- **Stay Motivated**—Realize that there is a vast difference between wishing for something and doing what is necessary to achieve it. Visualize the ways in which your life will change for the better as soon as you start achieving your objectives. You will have more success in making your dreams come true if you have a vivid picture of them in your mind.
- **Strive for Excellence**—Be the best that you can be in everything you do.
- **Be Flexible**—Alter your goals and timelines whenever necessary to meet new realities. If your personal or family situation changes and a specific goal is no longer feasible, or if there is a change in the financial markets that is beyond your control, set a new goal to meet the changing situation.
- **Be Realistic**—Set reasonable and achievable objectives. Don't aim for goals that you know are totally unrealistic given your age, your health, family responsibilities, or the maximum amount you can expect to invest, etc.
- **Be Persistent**—Don't cave in, don't give up—be persistent. Lack of persistence is one of the major causes of failure.
- **Take Action, Become Action–Oriented**—If you don't take the necessary steps to achieve your goals, everything else is a waste of time. Begin slowly, in small stages, but do begin, without further delay.

The Secret of Investment Success—Getting Started

The most important, and perhaps the most difficult, step is still ahead of you: getting started with your investments, actually sitting down and determining how much you will be able to invest weekly or monthly, and putting your funds into the best investment options. As you begin to set up your own savings and investment plan, you may have a number of basic and practical questions that need answering. Some of these questions will include:

- What is the best and fastest way for the average person to achieve wealth today—through increased earnings in a job or career, through a full-time or part-time business or franchise opportunity, through savings or investments, or some other way?
- What are the most viable investment options for persons who are already in their forties or fifties—mutual funds, stocks, bonds, real estate, art and antiques, or collectibles?
- What does a person need to know or learn to become a savvy investor?
- How can my family and I begin to save more and to invest more?
- How do *I* get started?

Consumer Debt—The Scourge of the Baby Boomers?

The older and more mature Baby Boomers are now entering what is called their "savings mode"—in which they are beginning to sock away or invest a substantial amount of money for their retirement—but a large number of Boomers carry a heavy load of debt. Many Boomers grew up during the "age of acquisition" in which they bought anything they wanted (homes, cars, boats, the latest electronic equipment, etc.) by charging it and a substantial number of Boomers still adhere to the "spend now, worry later" way of life. As a result of this laissez-faire attitude, however, many Boomers are in deep financial trouble.

It's rather ironic that almost everyone in a financial strait, no matter what their income level, believes that they could get out of debt and live well if only they had a higher income. The person earning $500 or $600 a week laments the fact that he or she isn't earning $1,000 a week; individuals earning $1,000 weekly are convinced they'd never be in debt again if only they could earn $1,500 or $2,000 per week, and so it goes. The simple fact is, people at each and every income level fail to make ends meet because the larger the income, the larger the expenditures. In almost every instance, they are spending far more than they earn.

What is required, no matter what the salary level actually is, is a written budget or spending plan and some smart money management. To get out of debt and become financially independent, you must make the management and control of your finances a primary concern.

How Do You Know if You've Maxed Out on Credit?

The danger signals are many and most of them are rather obvious. Ask yourself the following questions:

Financial Distress—Level 1
- Do I pay all my bills monthly or do I juggle and pay only some of them?
- Do I take cash advances from one credit card account to pay the monthly minimum on another account?
- Do I take cash advances to pay my rent or my utility or telephone bills?
- When my bills come in, do I open them or do I ignore them by stuffing them into a folder or drawer to deal with later?
- Do I consider it a "miracle" when I get a solicitation in the mail from a bank offering me another "prequalified" charge card with a large line of credit?

Financial Distress—Level 2
- Are one or more of my automobiles in danger of being repossessed?
- Will I have to take out a second mortgage or refinance my first mortgage in order not to lose my home?
- Will I have to dip into my retirement fund to pay for my children's college education?

If you answered yes to most of these questions, you're already in a financial hole that may be difficult to escape from without a great deal of planning and cutting back.

Getting Out of Debt

There are at least four major areas of money distribution:

1. *Cash* for miscellaneous expenditures and incidentals.
2. A *checking account* for regular expenses (rent or mortgage payments, utilities, telephone, automobile or other transportation expenses, insurance, food and clothing, etc.).
3. A *savings account* for unexpected expenses or for larger purchases that you don't wish to charge in order to avoid interest. Most experts recommend that the bare minimum amount in your savings account, *at all times*, should be equivalent to at least three months' net income.
4. One or more investment accounts for your long-range goals (college education for your children, savings for your retirement, etc.).

The following steps are necessary to begin to get your finances in order:

- Work out a plan to pay off your debts as quickly as possible especially credit card or retail accounts that carry a high interest rate.
- Don't make any purchases that aren't absolutely necessary until your debts are paid. Put off buying that new car, electronic equipment, or computer system, etc., unless it is something that is vital for business.
- Pay with cash whenever possible; try not to make any new charges until your finances are stabilized again.
- Set up a budget or spending plan to control expenses and to help you save for specific purchases.
- Start a savings account, no matter how small, as soon as your debts are liquidated to avoid financial hardship in the future.

Begin the process by writing down all your expenditures for at least three months to get a clearer idea of where your money goes. (To make things easier, use the worksheet at the end of this chapter.)

Review your canceled checks and your credit card statements every month to make sure you haven't overlooked anything. Next, write down your anticipated net income for the next three months.

At the end of the three-month period, sit down and add the various expenses such as rent or mortgage payments, telephone, utilities, food, books, and entertainment expenses. Don't forget to include miscellaneous expenses for the small items, because over a period of time they add up.

Is Debt Consolidation a Good Idea?

Debt consolidation loans can be very helpful if you cannot meet your monthly payments. The one monthly payment will be lower than the total of all of your individual credit card payments. This loan makes it easier on your cash flow.

The disadvantage of such a loan is that the interest will probably be higher than the interest you were paying to the credit card companies, and you will probably have to repay a consolidation loan over a longer period of time than the credit card loans.

When Should You Consider Bankruptcy?

According to the American Bankruptcy Institute, more than 90 percent of personal bankruptcies are the result of excessive credit card debt. Try to avoid bankruptcy by consolidation of your loans. If you file for bankruptcy, your credit report will show this for seven years.

Your Credit Cards—Keep Them or Destroy Them?

Are you aware that it is no longer a status symbol to carry a lot of credit cards in your wallet or purse—even if they are gold, platinum, or silver in color. The reason for this is that so many of the "hoi polloi" (the masses, the riffraff) now have these so-called "prestige" cards, there's no longer anything prestigious about them. In fact, according to financial columnist Jane Bryant Quinn, paying cash has become the status symbol of the 1990s. She says it shows that "you have money enough not to take plastic seriously."

None of the experts, however, recommend that you cancel all of your credit cards—at least one or two pieces of plastic may be needed for convenience. It's almost impossible to rent a car, for example, without a credit card and putting travel expenses (airline tickets, hotel and restaurant charges, etc.) on a card is another convenience, especially if your expenses are reimbursable or deductible. In addition, as more and more people shop from specialty catalogues by phone or over the Internet, a charge card or a bank debit card will be a necessity.

How Many Credit Cards Do You Need?

Jane Bryant Quinn recommends only two credit cards for the majority of us:

- A *"convenience"* card that has a small annual fee and a grace period before interest starts accumulating—for all smaller purchases and charges that can be paid in full at the end of each month; and
- A *low-interest card*—for larger purchases that will take a few months or longer to pay off.

Because so many banks are now charging high annual fees just to have one of their cards and have eliminated the grace period (which means that interest starts accumulating as soon as you make your purchase), some financial experts recommend that you eliminate the convenience charge card completely and use a bank debit card instead. There are advantages and disadvantages to this approach (see the section on *Bank Debit Cards*).

Although a low-interest credit card is desirable for larger purchases, you may have to shop around to get such a card, especially if you have a checkered payment history—you pay your bills on time for a few months, and then you get a little behind and pay them late for a few months.

Bank Debit Cards—Convenience or Headache?

Although most banks charge a low monthly fee (the average is about $1.00 per month) for unlimited use of their debit cards, it's not always advantageous to use a bank debit card instead of a conventional charge card. First of all, of course, you must already have the money in your bank account when you make any purchases with your bank debit card because the total expenditure will be deducted from your account immediately or within twenty-four hours.

Another disadvantage of the debit card is that if it is lost or stolen and used by someone else, your bank account can be wiped out rather quickly. It may take several days to get the problem straightened out with your bank.

Banks that issue debit cards have strict rules and regulations about what is covered if your card is used fraudulently and how soon you have to report a lost or stolen card. In most cases, your liability is no more than $50 if you inform your bank within a specified number of days. You would be well advised to know your own bank's regulations in this regard.

If you use your debit card frequently, it's a good idea not to wait until you get your monthly statement to determine if any erroneous transactions have been deducted from your account. Occasionally, a purchase will be deducted twice (or not at all), and your account will thus show an inaccurate balance. You can use your bank's 800 number to obtain information about your account on a regular basis.

Also, keep all of your debit card receipts, at least until your get your monthly statement, even if they are for only small amounts from the supermarket, drugstore, or similar outlets. It's often these small amounts that people forget to deduct from their balance when they use their debit card. Needless to say, this can cause havoc, especially if you maintain a small balance in your checking account.

There is at least one, even more important, disadvantage in using a bank debit card instead of a conventional credit card. Although purchases are deducted from your account immediately, returned items are not always credited back to your account immediately. This might become a problem, for example, if you use your debit card for an expensive purchase that you had to return. It may take several days before the bank's computer is able to put the money back into your account.

On the other hand, if you had used a regular credit card for this purchase and you returned the item, you would not have had to wait to get the funds back into your account. They would not have left your account in the first place and you would have avoided all this hassle. The small amount of interest you would have to pay for charging the item and paying the bill as soon as you received your statement might be well worth it in the long run.

What's the Real Scoop on Secured Credit Cards?

A "secured" Visa or MasterCard may be the only credit card available to those people with no credit or poor credit (for whatever reason) or for those who have been through a bankruptcy. In order to be issued a secured card, you will have to make a deposit of a minimum amount (usually $200) into a special savings account set up by the bank issuing the card or one of its affiliates.

Some banks require that you deposit 100 percent of your desired credit line into the savings account. Other banks will give a secured card holder a credit line that is twice your savings account deposit, so you might be asked to deposit only $250 for a $500 credit line. You should check around and see what the specific rules and requirements are for each bank offering this type of Visa or MasterCard. In any case, your deposit will be held as collateral in an interest-bearing account, and you won't be able to touch it for a stated period of time (usually at least one year) or until you cancel your secured credit card.

Your secured card can be used the same as any other charge card. If you default or get behind on your monthly payments, the bank has the right to seize the funds you deposited into the special savings account to cover your outstanding charges.

Having access to a secured credit card is a godsend for many people, but there are definite disadvantages. The following fees usually apply to a secured card:

- An application fee (usually $25 to $75).
- A high interest rate on your card purchases (more than 20 percent annually) while receiving a small percent annually for your collateral deposit.

- An annual processing fee ($50 or more).
- Additional monthly fees if your payment is a day or two late or if you exceed your credit limit by a few dollars. If this happens frequently with your account, you may end up paying quite a lot of money each month in addition to the normal minimum interest.

At this point, you may be wondering if there are any advantages in having a secured credit card, especially since you have to come up with the cash to get the card in the first place. The advantages are these:

- If you have poor credit or no credit and you can't get a credit card any other way, a secured card helps you to reestablish your credit worthiness. However, you must make your monthly payments in a timely manner—there's no point in going to all the trouble of getting a secured card and damaging your credit rating even further by paying late.
- If you make timely payments—especially if you pay more than the minimum each month—within a year or two the bank issuing you the secured card may be willing to return your savings deposit to you and issue you a regular Visa or MasterCard. Or they may increase your credit line without asking you for an additional deposit into the savings account.

If you are interested in a secured credit card, call your local banks to see if they issue such cards. Many of them do, even if they don't advertise the fact. To obtain a list of banks nationwide that issue secured cards, write to:

Bankcard Holders of America
560 Herndon Parkway
Suite 120
Herndon, VA 22070

After you get the list, write to several different banks, requesting information about their secured cards. Be sure to read the information the banks send you very carefully before mailing in an application fee.

Tips for Smart Money Management

Tip # 1 —Save Thousands in Interest by Making Larger Payments on your Mortgage

You can cut years off your mortgage payments and save a small fortune in interest by making payments biweekly rather than monthly, or by making extra payments on the principal each month. The following chart shows how long it will take to pay off a thirty-year mortgage for $100,000 at 7.5 percent interest if you pay monthly, every two weeks (26 payments) per year, and if you add $25.00 or $50.00 to each biweekly payment.

If your bank will not set up a biweekly payment schedule, write two checks each month—one check for your regular payment and a second check for the "principal only" portion that you want to pay. It is estimated that every extra dollar put into your mortgage in the early years may save you around three dollars in the future.

The experts recommend that you steer clear of promoters who, for a hefty fee, will accelerate your mortgage payments for you. You don't need them, you can do it yourself.

Tip # 2—Postpone Buying a New Car

Many people want to trade in their car for a newer model as soon as they get their current car loan paid off. If you keep your car for at

	Monthly	*Biweekly*	*+$25.00*	*+$50.00*
Payment of	$699.20	$352.11	$377.11	$402.11
Paid off in	30 years	23.5 years	19.8 years	17.3 years
Interest paid	$151,719	$112,658	$92,162	$78,513
Interest Savings	—	$39,061	$59,557	$73,206

least a couple more years and put the equivalent of those monthly car payments into a savings account, you will be very pleasantly surprised to find an additional $8,000 to $12,000 in your savings account at the end of only two short years.

Tip # 3—**Review Your Credit Report on a Regular Basis**

Make a habit of requesting a copy of your credit report at least once a year to ensure that no erroneous information has been put into your file. What many people don't realize is that a credit bureau is nothing more than an agency that gathers and reports data on millions and millions of people. It does not evaluate your credit worthiness and does not approve or disapprove credit and loan applications.

The credit bureau will send out a copy of your file to banks, stores, credit card companies, etc., upon request, but the bureau has no way of determining whether the information that has been entered into your file is accurate. It is your responsibility to check it periodically to see that it is. One of the most troublesome errors and often the hardest to rectify, is when two people have the exact same name and information about either of them is put into the wrong file. It can be especially troublesome to the individual with "perfect credit" when someone else's bad credit reports are entered into his record.

The three major credit bureaus are:

Equifax Credit Information Services
1-800-711-5341

Experian Credit Information Services
1-888-397-3742

Trans Union Corporation
1-800-645-1533

Depending on which state you live in, you can request a credit report from the "big three" at no cost or only a nominal charge. When you call their 800 numbers, you may be able to punch in the necessary information on your touch-tone phone and in less than a week you will receive your credit reports.

After your receive your reports, review them carefully. Keep in mind that negative, but accurate, information about your credit habits will remain in the report for seven years, and information about any bankruptcies or tax liens will stay in the file for ten years. Along with your credit report you will receive an information sheet telling you how to correct erroneous or disputed information. Don't delay in correcting any obvious errors. Also, don't hesitate to write a concise explanation of why you might have gotten behind on some of your payments in the past (illness, unemployment, etc.); this explanation will become part of your file.

Tip # 4—Stay Away from Credit Repair Clinics

These companies are considered vultures because they charge exorbitant fees and claim they can repair a bad credit history. Don't believe them for a minute. They can't make the negative information in your credit file disappear unless it is inaccurate, and you can do that yourself with a letter to the credit bureau(s). Accurate information, no matter how negative it is, cannot be legally removed from your credit file for seven years.

Tip # 5—Consult a Credit Counseling Service if You Get in a Financial Bind

Be sure not to confuse a dishonest credit repair service with a legitimate credit counseling service. A credit counseling agency offers a valuable service to the individual or family in temporary financial straits. In addition to providing moral support when you need it most, they will review your financial situation and help you work out a smaller payment schedule with your creditors.

Credit counseling services are non-profit organizations, and they charge only a modest monthly or one-time fee. For the name and phone number of a non-profit counseling service in your community, call your local department of social services or the National Foundation for Consumer Credit at 1-800-284-1723.

Tip # 6—Examine Your Attitudes Towards Money

It is important to examine your early childhood experiences to try and determine your subconscious feelings about money. Some people grow up with a religious attitude that was taken from the Bible, which says that the love of money is the root of all evil. One outstanding minister, Rev. Eikerenkoetter, said that the Apostle Paul has it wrong—it is the lack of money that is the root of all evil. Nevertheless, some people have developed some attitudes about money that may be keeping money away from them. Remember everything begins in the mind.

Some individuals believe that if a person drives an expensive automobile and has a large, beautiful home, that person must have acquired his wealth illegally. When a wealthy person commits suicide, some people will say that money doesn't buy happiness. They overlook the fact that many poor people commit suicide also.

Some people even pray for only a limited amount of money by saying "Lord, I don't want a lot of money. I just want enough to pay my bills."

Your state of mind has a direct effect on your finances. If you have a negative or indifferent attitude toward money, it is important that you create a positive message for reprogramming your subconscious mind. Use the methods mentioned in this book such as saying a positive affirmation to yourself on a daily basis. Use positive statements about money to replace any fears or negative thoughts that you have about money.

The ABCs of Money Management

A. Every Baby Boomer should have two sources of income: an earned income and an investment income.
B. Build a diversified investment portfolio. You do not become wealthy on the money you work for. It's the money that works for you that makes the difference.
C. People who are successful are those who do what they know best. Therefore, do what you know best.

To protect the purchasing power of your lifetime savings from deteriorating through inflation, it is necessary for you to invest and participate in growth of the economy. Your journey to wealth can begin as you take control of your personal finances and control negative spending habits.

Determine your net worth by completing the form on the following page.

Financial Assets and Net Worth

Property Assets
Residence $_____
Vacation or second home $_____
Automobiles $_____
Furnishings $_____
Jewelry and art $_____
Other property assets $_____

Cash Reserve Assests
Checking accounts $_____
Savings accounts $_____
Certificates of deposit $_____
Other cash reserve assets $_____

Equity Assets
Real estate $_____
Stocks $_____
Mutual funds $_____
Variable annuities $_____
Life insurance with cash value $_____
IRA, SEP, 401(k) or 403(b) accounts $_____
Business interests $_____
Other equity assets $_____

Fixed Assets
Government bonds $_____
Municipal bonds $_____
Corporate bonds $_____
Face amount certificates $_____
Fixed annuities $_____
Other fixed assets $_____
                       Total Assets $_____

Liabilities
Home mortgage $_____
Other mortgages $_____
Auto loans $_____
Personal loans $_____
Charge and credit card accounts $_____
Other debts $_____
                    Total Liabilities $_____
Total assets $_____
Less total liabilities $_____
                     Your Net Worth $_____

Worksheet: Figuring Your Cash Flow

Monthly income

Wages, salary, tips	$_____
Dividends from stocks, mutual funds, etc.	$_____
Interest on savings accounts, CDs, etc.	$_____
Social Security	$_____
Pension income	$_____
Annuities	$_____
Other	$_____
Total Monthly Income	$_____

Monthly expenditures

Housing (includes rent or mortgage payments, property/real estate taxes, household maintenance)	$_____
Essentials (includes food, clothing, and medical and dental bills)	$_____
Taxes (includes income, property and Social Security taxes)	$_____
Utilities (includes gas, electric, telephone, etc.)	$_____
Transportation (includes car loans, gasoline, car maintenance, and plane, train, bus and taxi fares)	$_____
Leisure (includes entertainment, travel, vacation home mortgage, club dues)	$_____
Loan and installment payments (includes credit and charge card)	$_____
Insurance (includes health, homeowner's, life, long-term care)	$_____
Gifts, charitable contributions	$_____
Investments	$_____
Other expenses	$_____
Total Monthly Expenses	$_____

Net Cash Flow

Total monthly income	$_____
Less total monthly expenses	$_____
Your Discretionary Monthly Income	$_____

BABY BOOMER STRATEGY PLANNER

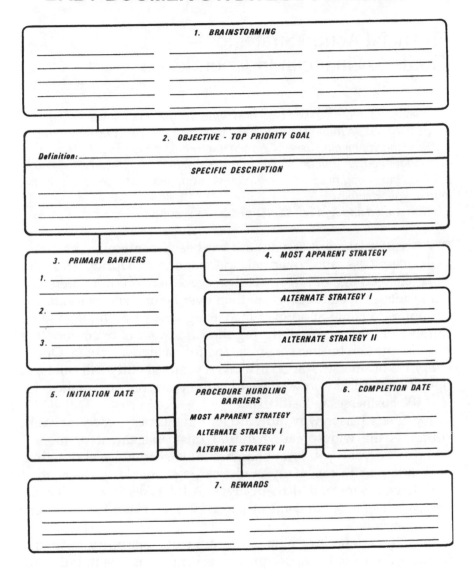

Chapter 12

Financial Action Strategies—
Guide to Financial Independence

A young man once asked God how long a million years was to Him.
God replied, "A million years to me is just like a single second in your time."
Then the young man asked God what a million dollars was to Him.
God replied, "A million dollars to me is just like a single penny to you."
Then the young man got his courage up and asked, "God, could I have one of your pennies?"
God smiled and replied, "Certainly, just a second."

The eternal quest of mankind has been a continuing search for happiness and financial independence. During this un-equaled age of affluence, however, there are more personal bankruptcies in America today than ever before, and that number continues to climb at an ever-increasing rate. In addition, a large number of businesses fail during their first year of operation. In a recent report on business failures, the following was noted: Out of every 100 businesses started in a given year, only fifty will still be in operation the next year. At the end of ten years, only ten of the original 100 businesses will still exist.

A primary reason why individuals and businesses declare bankruptcy is the widespread, habitual mismanagement of money. Almost everyone you know has had money troubles at one time or another. With too many credit cards available to them, they may have overextended themselves. All it takes is a sudden illness, a loss of a job, or some other unforeseen event to wipe them out financially.

Even if they aren't verging on the point of bankruptcy, too many working adults fail to apply proven principles of wealth-building. Then, at age sixty-five, they find themselves burned out and lacking the financial resources to maintain their current lifestyle. They are totally unable to have the kind of retirement they have always dreamed about.

The insurance industry provides additional grim statistics. Less than 5 percent of the population at age sixty-five is financially independent. That means that nearly 95 percent of the people who have worked most of their adult lives do not have enough money to support themselves. They must, to one degree or another, rely on outside sources such as Social Security, relatives, friends, charity, or part-time jobs during the twilight of life.

Why is this the case? How can you prevent this from happening in your own life? In this chapter, we will give you some of the answers.

Like many other people, you may not have given much thought to the meaning of financial independence, other than you hope to achieve it—someday. Up to this point, you may have been content simply to keep your head above water and to get your bills paid by their due date. However, the time has come to challenge yourself to take the steps that are necessary to reach financial success. There is no limit to the wealth that you can acquire. By applying the rules, principles, and concepts that have made others wealthy, you will develop financial independence for yourself and your family.

It is important at this point that you begin considering specific goals that will ensure your financial independence. Begin to see yourself as financially independent now. Realize that nothing—not your employer, not the general conditions of the marketplace, not the daily ups and downs of the stock market—stands between you and financial success.

Success is no accident. Failure is no accident. Learning the habits of financial success and independence is no different than learning any other good habit. Money is basically nothing more than an abstract concept, at best semi-tangible. Take a dollar bill or any other piece of money and examine it. Can you eat it? Will it keep you warm on a cold winter's night? Can it be used as structural material in building a new home? The answer, of course, is no. Money is only an idea, a concept, a tool, something to control and not something that should ever control you. Its value rests only in the faith placed in it by you and the business world in which you exchange it. Money must be spent, it must be exchanged for something of far greater intrinsic value.

Financial independence is the acquisition of enough income-producing sources, whether in real estate, stocks and bonds, businesses, or any of dozens of other possible areas, that will provide you with your desired standard of living, both now and in the future. Making money work for you, instead of you working for money, is what creates wealth. The proper manipulation of wealth is what evolves into financial independence. With financial independence, you need not depend upon or fear anyone else's power, decisions, or actions.

Getting Rid of Your Negative Concepts about Wealth

One of the first false concepts about money that needs to be put to rest is the widespread belief that accumulating wealth and financial independence causes a person to become avaricious and dishonest. This is hardly ever the case. In fact, just the opposite may occur. When you no longer have to worry about paying your bills or how you are going to survive after retirement, your entire outlook on life improves and you can begin to make the lives of others a little brighter by contributing to your favorite neighborhood church or charity. You can even give more of yourself through volunteer work. None of that would be possible if you were still living from paycheck to paycheck, still grubbing for money just to make ends meet.

Getting rid of your negative concepts about money is a strong first step toward financial independence.

Pay Yourself First

Now let's look at another aspect of using money. Ask yourself the question, Who comes first? In a little story entitled "The Richest Man in Babylon," (Clason, 1955) the key message is that a portion of all you earn is yours to keep. In other words, each time you receive a pay check, commission check from your job or profession, or take your salary as profits from your own business, the first person to pay with that money is *you*. Pay yourself by taking a portion of your income and immediately setting it aside for savings or investment regardless of your credit standing, financial pressures, or any other monetary commitment. This rule must never be broken, no matter how tempting it may be at times to "skip" a payment to yourself.

This principle and its ramifications must be clearly and firmly set in your mind and in your actions for the rest of your life if you are to gain financial independence. Regardless of bills on your desk, mortgage payments due, or any other financial obligation, at least one-tenth of all your income must be set aside before paying anyone else. At least one-tenth must be put into some form of savings or investment plan.

Baby Boomers and the Importance of Brainstorming

To become financially independent, you must have a reason, you must have a burning desire for the end result. These reasons and desires are the vehicles that put you in a position to acquire or accomplish the things you want, the things that are the most important to you by your own personal values.

Brainstorming has proven time and time again to be highly effective in the business world, and is now proving equally productive in areas of personal achievement and success. There are two basic rules of brainstorming. First, record any and every idea that comes up. Second, do not qualify or consider a negative factor that you think may hinder your strivings. Give no thought to any reason for the idea not becoming a reality.

It is extremely important that you picture what you want. Create the distinct imprint of your aspirations in your mind. Crystallize in your thoughts exactly what you will gain. Then, you will build these ideas into realities. You will know what you want out of life, and you will achieve it. By following these principles and procedures, you are giving yourself reasons and motivational goals to use as building blocks in your quest for financial independence. Without reasons and goals, why should you proceed any further? "Where there is no vision," the Scriptures read, "the people perish." (Proverbs 29:18)

If you look at the biographies of wealthy and well-known personalities, it will become apparent that each one found his own road to financial success. Different areas of business and investment were used as tools by different people. For some, such as Donald Trump, it was real estate. For Bill Gates and Michael Dell, it was computers and computer technology. For Michael Eisner and Steven Spielberg, it was the entertainment industry. These individuals and thousands more like them throughout America, did not inherit their fortunes but created them with their own talents and abilities.

The chances are excellent that the source of your own wealth is to be found in the creativity of your mind. You don't have to go looking for some "get-rich-quick" scheme. Your vehicle to monetary freedom is probably available to you right now. Apply the principles and methods outlined in this chapter to the opportunities presented through your present job, to investment opportunities you might know of, and to dozens of other timely offerings that will inevitably pop up in your life if you just keep your mind and eyes open.

Developing Financial Maturity and Using Credit Profitably

An essential element for financial maturity is knowing your exact financial status. You must know your assets and liabilities, your income and expenditures, and your overhead. (To assess your personal net worth, complete the Net Worth form at the end of chapter 11.)

You also need to know when to spend your money and when not to spend it. Unusual investment opportunities become available occasionally, but they are not everyday occurrences. For each profitable investment, fifty never earn any money. The financially mature individual always considers each proposition carefully. The best rule of thumb is, "If you can't afford to lose the money, don't play the game." Speculations are ideal if you can use them as a tax write-off, but if a total bust would put you near bankruptcy, pass it up.

Credit is still one of the most important tools for building financial independence. Few people have reached their financial goals without extensive use of credit. In mastering the use of this tool, however, they have taken great pains to establish a solid record, thus proving to the business world that they are financially mature. In the modem world of business and finance, it is almost impossible to become wealthy and independent without establishing good credit, and after establishing it, using it.

Remember, credit is nothing more than a commodity. It is sold, and it is purchased. As with any other product, careful shopping can bring a superior bargain. Examination of terms and creditors can mean the difference between profit and loss. A wise investor examines every facet of a loan before he or she signs on the dotted line.

If you should find yourself or your company in serious debt, the first thing to do is to make certain that your creditors know where you are and how you can be reached. This curbs the likelihood of legal action. Second, work out a financial plan with a professional accountant to determine how you will pay your creditors and still retain an adequate income. This will show your creditors that you mean business and, at the same time, will cut off the flow of collection calls and letters.

Using Other People's Money

There are several ways of using other people's money (OPM), and some of them are profitable while others are not. While the routine uses of credit by the consumer are usually nonprofitable, the use of OPM may be a highly profitable application of the credit concept. In general, you will not find many wealthy and financially independent people who have not borrowed money, or who have not used OPM at one time or another to make more money. The use of OPM will take a different form for different people in different enterprises, but it is always there someplace, and it is always an integral part of the financial success of wealthy men. Proper use of OPM requires intelligence, integrity, good credit, patience, and a sound plan. If you are willing to employ these factors, your wealth and financial independence are assured.

You can also create your own money machine. There are basically two types of money machines. The first one you operate yourself, such as your own business or profession. The second is one into which you invest money, and it operates for you without your immediate involvement. Typical of this type of money machine are investments in the stock market, in real estate, or in businesses in which you have no responsibility regarding their day-to-day operations.

The Three Keys to Successful Investment

There are three keys to successful investment.

First, learn as much as possible about the investment area that interests you.

Second, qualify all advice you receive concerning your proposed investments. The best advice comes from experts, people who have trained and specialized in a particular field.

Third, never turn your capital over to someone who is not fully qualified to handle it. The moment you release your money to be managed by someone else, you are taking a chance. The wisest thing to do to reduce your risk is to place your money in the hands of an expert if you are not qualified to do it yourself.

Remember that the money you set aside from your earnings for investments is your financial future in the making. You have worked hard for it. The same maturity and objectivity must be used to invest successfully to increase your wealth even further. Do not delegate the responsibility of multiplying your capital to someone else. If you decide to invest in stocks and bonds, be active in supervising your portfolio. If you choose real estate, you are as much at fault as the broker if a bad investment is made. In other words, no matter what areas you decide to invest in, be forever vigilant and train yourself to know what is happening.

The Stock Markets

One of the most frequently used money machines is the formalized trading market such as the stock market. Stock markets, of one sort or another, go back many centuries. Derivation of the word stems from the ancient market places where cattle, pigs, sheep, and other stock were traded. There are stock markets throughout the world today, including many in the United States. The New York Stock Exchange, the American Stock Exchange, and Nasdaq are the best known in the United States. Other exchanges operate in Boston, Philadelphia, Chicago, San Francisco, Los Angeles, and other American cities. Still more are to be found in London, Tokyo, and dozens of other cities around the world. Some of these markets, such as the

New York Stock Exchange, handle only the securities of listed corporations, while other exchanges deal in a much more diverse spectrum of finance.

Rather than enter the stock market with limited knowledge, many individuals turn their money over to a management group. Organizations known as mutual funds form a fiduciary contract with the investors and use their cash for stock purchases. This method allows the private citizen to build a diversified portfolio of bonds, stocks, and municipal securities without the high expenditure or great risk of personal investment.

In some areas of the country, investment in real estate is still one of the most attractive vehicles for large capital gains. In other areas, however, the annual return from real estate investments is hardly more than what you might receive from a Certificate of Deposit (CD). Although land does not diminish in value, commercial property, office buildings, and homes sometimes do or else they require a considerable amount of capital for renovation and repair before they can be resold. Depending on where you live and the type of real estate investment you choose, you should consider the prospective real estate investment very carefully before putting a large portion of your capital into it.

* * *

Life is not an end in itself, but rather an exciting journey. Your journey toward financial independence will provide much pleasure if you plan for it with optimism, enthusiasm, and a small dose of realism. Don't expect to just wake up one morning to find yourself as rich as Donald Trump or Michael Dell or Bill Gates. Know who you are and what you want out of life. As you challenge yourself every day to achieve your long-term goals, including the things you want when you eventually retire, your immediate reward will be increased happiness and peace of mind.

Why Baby Boomers Should Plan for Retirement Now

As Baby Boomers enjoy the peak years of their earning power and careers, retirement may seem far off, but for the first Boomers the traditional retirement age of sixty-five is less than fifteen years away. Even the younger Baby Boomers are at an age where saving for retirement is crucial. Consider these facts: (Berger, 1988)

- People are retiring earlier and living longer, healthier lives. It is not uncommon now to live past the age of ninety. As a result, you can expect to spend at least a quarter of your life (twenty years or more) in retirement.
- Social Security provides less than half the income of today's retirees and is expected to provide proportionately less in the future.
- Traditional, lifetime, company-provided pensions are becoming less common.

Whatever your current age may be, it is important that you organize your financial plans for retirement now and get them into action without further delay. Planning is actually much easier than you might think. The sooner you start, the easier it will be to succeed. There are several reasons to start planning for retirement now:

Americans are living longer. This may be one of those "good news, bad news" situations. The good news is that Baby Boomers are expected to live longer than their parents and grandparents. The bad news is, can they afford to live longer? Will Social Security, retirement pension(s), investments, and savings be enough to provide them with more than the necessities?

Americans are getting healthier. You may enjoy a more active lifestyle than your parents and grandparents, which also will require more available funds to enjoy those extra, and healthier, years of your life.

Inflation appears to be a permanent reality on the world economic scene. Although the current (1999) inflation rate is near zero, don't expect it to forever remain so. Even a modest rise in inflation each year over the projected twenty or thirty years of your retirement may seriously diminish your retirement nest egg.

As Baby Boomers grow closer to retirement age, they are realizing they cannot rely on the government as a primary source of finan-

cial support. To be on the safe side when you plan for retirement, count less on Social Security, Medicare, and other governmental support and rely more on your own efforts for financial security in retirement.

How Much Will Baby Boomers Need to Retire with Confidence?

According to *U.S. News & World Report,* today's 40-year-old will need to accumulate $1.7 million by age sixty-five to provide an annual retirement income of $35,000 from age sixty-five to age ninety.

Costs that may *decrease* for retired Baby Boomers include the following:

Taxes. You'll probably be earning less, so your income taxes will be lower. Also, you may not be paying employment taxes.

Mortgage payments. You may have paid off your mortgage or may decide to move into a smaller home, as many retirees do.

Job-related expenses. You won't need to pay for the high cost of commuting, for business attire, restaurant meals, personal care, and other expenses that you incur as part of your full-time occupation.

Education costs. Your children will probably have finished college or graduate school by the time you retire.

Loan repayments and interest. You'll be making fewer costly purchases, so you'll pay less interest and sales taxes.

Life insurance. Most life insurance policies are paid up by age sixty-five, and those with cash value start paying you.

Costs that may *increase* for retired Baby Boomers:

Health care costs. As we all know, health care costs are constantly rising and as you approach retirement, your need for medical care may also increase.

Recreation and entertainment expenses. As a retiree you will have more leisure time to travel, read, enjoy cultural activities, etc., all of which may take a larger portion of your budget than when you were employed and had little time for travel and entertainment.

General cost of living expenses. Food, utilities, and other basic necessities may become more expensive.

What Can Baby Boomers Expect from Social Security?

If you're paying Social Security taxes now on a gross annual salary in the neighborhood of $45,000, you will receive approximately $10,000 annually in Social Security benefits. For annual earnings between $18,000 and $45,000, the figure falls between $7,500 and $10,000. The exact amount will be calculated by the Social Security Administration according to a formula based on contributions you've made, and the age at which you plan to retire. Your Social Security check will not meet all your needs, but it can provide a base for your retirement plan.

At the standard retirement age of sixty-five (which will be increased gradually to age sixty-seven by the year 2027), you can receive the full benefits you're qualified for. If you retire early, between the age of sixty-two and the standard age, the amount of your monthly check will be reduced, and the reduction is permanent.

Other Sources of Retirement Income

The most common types of retirement income other than Social Security include funds received from pension plans, income from rental properties, dividends and royalties, life insurance annuities, interest income from investments, and payments for working part-time. Tax-deferred savings vehicles should be the cornerstone of your retirement planning. You probably have access to some tax-deferred retirement plan through your employer, such as a 401(k), 403(B) or 457 plan. If you are self-employed, you may have a Keogh or profit-sharing plan. More than ever, an Individual Retirement Plan (IRA) is one of the best ways to save for retirement.

The IRA is one of the few remaining tax-deferred retirement saving investments available to everyone. Beginning in 1998, new Federal legislation expands deductibility and creates new deductions, each with different tax advantages and eligibility rules.

IRAs at a Glance

Deductible IRAs

- A nonworking person can qualify for a contribution deduction if his or her spouse has a pension plan and the joint income is below $150,000.
- The income cap for deductions gradually increases to $50,000 (for individuals) and $80,000 (for couples) if the employed individual is covered by a qualified plan.
- Penalty-free withdrawal for qualified first-time home purchases or education expenses (normal income taxes will apply).

Roth IRAs (new nondeductible IRAs)

- May contribute up to $2,000 of earned income.
- Income must be $100,000 or below (individuals and couples) to be eligible for contributions.
- Earnings grow tax-free.
- Distribution will be completely tax-free if certain requirements are met.
- Funds can be accessed for certain qualified expenses, including first-time home purchases and education, as well as certain health insurance, medical and disability expenses.
- Can convert existing, traditional IRA to Roth IRA.

Education IRA (new nondeductible IRA)

- May contribute $500 per year per child until child turns eighteen.
- Contributions are not tax-deductible, but earnings are tax free.
- No tax on withdrawals, provided funds are used to pay for qualified higher education expenses for the child (tuition, fees, books, basic room and board, etc.).
- Account may be transferred for the benefit of another family member.
- Eligibility phases out with annual gross income of $95,000 (individuals), or $150,000 (couples).

If you have a pension plan through your employer, you will receive a fixed amount on a regular basis. You'll need to know how much you will receive monthly from this source so that you can begin planning your retirement investment program.

The sooner you begin an investment program, the longer you will have to achieve your goals with less effort and resources. That's because over time even the smallest amount saved can become a substantial amount, due to the power of compounding.

Whatever your financial goals—college education for your children, assisted living care for an elderly parent, or early retirement for yourself and your spouse—you can take a few steps now to get started on the road to success. If you have not yet opened an account with a stock broker, you should do so as soon as possible and continue to set aside a certain amount every month or every quarter to build up your investment account.

The following long-term investment strategies are recommended for building and maintaining wealth:

Guard Against Inflation

One of the biggest threats to your investment dollars is inflation. To ensure that you'll have the money you want in the future, you need an investment that will grow faster than the rate of inflation. After all, if the cost of living is higher than your investment return, you aren't making money—you're losing it. While today's inflation rate is relatively stable, even a modest rate of inflation can severely erode your purchasing power. The best way to tell whether or not your investments are beating inflation is to look at your "real" return (i.e., your total return minus the rate of inflation).

Historically, stocks have been the most effective way for investors to protect their money's long-term purchasing power. That is because only stocks have historically posted returns greater than the rate of inflation over the past seven decades. However, as with all investments, there are risks. In the case of stocks, that risk is price volatility.

As a Baby Boomer, you are in a unique position to take advantage of the wealth-building potential of stocks, because time is on your side. Generally, the more time you have to hold your equity investments, the greater the possibility you will experience positive returns. Since 1960, the Standard & Poors 500 has increased in value

94 percent of the time during five-year holding periods and 100 percent of the time during holding periods of ten years or longer.

Minimize Your Tax Payments

The time-honored way to build wealth over the long term is to invest in the stock market by purchasing individual stocks or shares in a stock mutual fund.

The upside: You have excellent potential for superior long-term returns. The downside: You risk losing up to nearly one-third to taxes. What can you do to minimize the effects of taxation on your investment portfolio?

1. Take advantage of as many tax-deferred retirement options as possible. Invest the maximum, if you can.
2. Hold stocks for more than 18 months before selling to take advantage of the new, lower 20 percent capital gains tax rate.
3. Consider diversifying a portion of your nonretirement portfolio in a tax-free municipal bond fund.
4. Offset gains with losses in the same tax year.
5. Consult with an account executive as well as a tax advisor.

Mutual Funds Can Help You Reach Your Financial Goals

Choosing the right investments for your financial needs is difficult for even the most experienced investor. That's why many people take advantage of mutual funds. Here's just a few of their major benefits and characteristics:

Diversification. Mutual funds provide instant diversification because a fund's portfolio is spread among many different securities. Since a mutual fund may invest in hundreds of different securities, a decline in the value of one may be offset by a rise in another.

Professional Management. Mutual funds are managed by financial experts who buy and sell securities for the fund's portfolio. The fund's managers have the resources and expertise to benefit individual investors who may not have the time, know-how, resources, or inclination to study the markets and select individual securities on their own.

Liquidity. Mutual fund shares provide a liquidity that is hard to match with any other investment. Fund shares can be purchased or sold easily and at any time. Of course, depending on market conditions, shares may be worth more or less than their original cost upon redemption.

Estate Planning. Estate planning today has assumed an increasing relevance and importance for the average American because of longer life expectancies. Estate planning typically takes the form of identifying and selecting from a variety of available legal and financial devices.

The following are suggested goals to create the objectives for your estate plan:

1. Avoid probate, which means, in essence, staying away from high court costs and attorney fees involved in having to probate your estate.
2. Minimize the possibility of taxes that may be levied against your estate after your death.
3. Arrange for proper distribution of your property upon death, and for proper care, guidance, and maintenance of any juveniles and/or other dependents upon your death.

Do not overlook the importance of having a will, even if it is only a few pages in length and is stated in simple, nonlegalistic terms. A will can be used to effect proper disposal of your property and affairs after your death. It also makes provisions for the care and maintenance of children or loved ones in your care. A "living will" can be used to provide for your health care and day-to-day management of your financial affairs during the term of any disabling illness.

You should also consider a "living trust," which means making gifts of your property while you are still alive, within special legal limits, setting up joint ownership of property and assets, and naming beneficiaries on savings bonds, life insurance policies, and/or employee retirement funds plans.

What all these devices can do is help you retain as much of your estate as possible, with the least amount of legal fees and other costs.

BABY BOOMER STRATEGY PLANNER

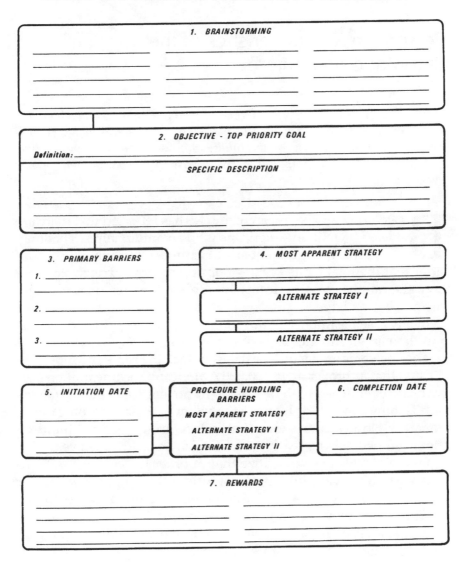

1. BRAINSTORMING

2. OBJECTIVE - TOP PRIORITY GOAL

Definition:

SPECIFIC DESCRIPTION

3. PRIMARY BARRIERS

1.

2.

3.

4. MOST APPARENT STRATEGY

ALTERNATE STRATEGY I

ALTERNATE STRATEGY II

5. INITIATION DATE

PROCEDURE HURDLING BARRIERS

MOST APPARENT STRATEGY

ALTERNATE STRATEGY I

ALTERNATE STRATEGY II

6. COMPLETION DATE

7. REWARDS

Chapter 13

Personality Characteristics of the Self-Made Millionaire

"The secret [to becoming a millionaire] is to put money somewhere that it will grow without your having to pay taxes on it immediately. We tell people that if they want to be the millionaire down the street by the time they're 50 or 55, they should put away at least 15 percent of their income every year."[1]

Based on extensive research, the IRS has reported that there are at least 1.8 million Americans who are millionaires. That may sound like a large number of rich folks, but when you consider that the total United States population now exceeds 265 million, the number of American who are millionaires doesn't really seem to be *that* large.

In any case the important question is, is it still possible to become a millionaire in America today?

The answer is an unequivocal yes! In fact, the same IRS report indicated that approximately 100,000 Americans become millionaires each and every year. With this fact in mind, naturally the next question is, how can you or I, an average Sam or Susan, become a millionaire? How can we join that select group of one hundred thousand people who reach the million dollar mark each year?

First of all, we need to realize that in order to become a millionaire, we don't have to inherit a trust fund from our grandparents or parents and we don't have to have a Ph.D. in economics, nor do we need to be employed as an executive with a Wall Street firm or a large national or multinational corporation and entitled to such perks as big bonuses and stock options.

According to the best-selling book, *The Millionaire Next Door: The Surprising Secrets of America's Wealthy* by William D. Danko and

---

[1] From an interview with Thomas J. Stanley, co-author of "The Millionaire Next Door," appearing in *U.S. News & World Report*, June 9, 1997.

Thomas J. Stanley, many of the new millionaires are self-employed in such diverse businesses as roofing contractors, scrap-metal dealers, owners of convenience marts, or fast food franchises.

What are some of the specific characteristics shared by the most successful men and women in America, those who have acquired wealth through their own efforts and ingenuity? What talents or traits do they have in common that enabled them to achieve extraordinary financial success? Without exception, people who have become rich and successful seem to share the following characteristics:

- *Intelligence.* Intelligence here is defined as a way of acting rather than an IQ score or a high grade-point average in college or graduate school. Many millionaires with limited formal education engage in very intelligent behavior. On the other hand, many people from the best colleges and with high IQs engage in unintelligent behavior. The definition of intelligent behavior refers to any action that moves you in the direction of something you want. Unintelligent or "stupid" behavior is any action that moves you away from something you want.

- *Self-discipline.* The most successful people are better disciplined than people who are unsuccessful and unhappy. This one quality, self-discipline, has been a critical factor in success throughout the ages. Self-discipline has been defined as the ability to make yourself do what you should do when you should do it, whether you like it or not. The achievers in life have developed the strength of will to do what others don't like to do by going the extra mile and fighting an uphill battle with themselves.

- *Love of work.* Successful people and self-made millionaires do the type of work they love to do for the joy of it. They tend to do more work than what they are paid to do. They are curious, interested, and open to new ideas and information.

- *Long-term perspective and the ability to visualize.* Dr. Edward Banfield of Harvard University analyzed more than fifty years of research to identify the success qualities of leaders. The one quality possessed by men and women who became leaders was long-term vision.

- *An attitude of self-employment.* It should be noted that many of the "millionaires next door" work for themselves, but even those who are employed by someone else have an attitude of self-employment. They look at everything that happens in the organization where they work as though it affects them personally.

- *An ability to bounce back after a defeat or disappointment.* Many self-made millionaires have tried a number of endeavors before they hit on the one that was the "big idea" for themselves.
- *A positive mental attitude.*
- *An ability to project forward to the future and then turn around and look back to the present.*

If *you* want to become a millionaire, do the following: (Tracy, 1997)

Dream big. Assume that you earn ten times your current income. What would you do? How would you act? What stands between you and your dream?

Focus on your unique strengths. We all have special talents and abilities that make us different from any other person. Identify your strengths and channel your efforts toward your goals.

See yourself as self-employed. If you are currently employed by someone else, act as if you own the business. The top 3 percent in every field have an attitude of self-employment. Look at everything that happens in your organization as though it affects you personally.

Never consider the possibility of failure. Be willing to take calculated risks to achieve greater rewards. The attitude toward risk taking is the most important indicator of your readiness to become wealthy. Look at failure as only another way of learning the lessons necessary to succeed.

Develop a clear sense of direction. "If you do not know where you are going, you will probably end up somewhere else." Set goals and make plans to accomplish them. (Tracy, 1997)

Work hard. Prepare yourself to work, work, work, work. On a normal workday when average Americans work eight hours a day, everything over eight hours is for success. Prepare yourself to put in a minimum of 80 hours a week if you intend to become wealthy. If you have clear goals, a dream, and are doing something you love, it will all come easy and you won't be aware of the extra 40 hours.

Associate with the right people. Successful people stick together. They avoid all negative situations, conversation, and people. Successful people help others who can help them in return.

Be teachable. If you want to achieve your full financial potential, you must be open to new information. Always question, and remain curious, interested, and open to new knowledge.

Be prepared to climb from peak to peak. Success is never one long, upward progression. Life is a series of ups and downs. Prepare for the coming winter even in the midst of a bountiful harvest, and plan for the spring and summer during the coldest days of winter.

Develop resilience and bounce back. In order to assure your success, you must have the ability to bounce back after a defeat or disappointment. We all face and meet setbacks and temporary failures in life.

Unlock your inborn creativity. Success is achieved by innovation, not copying. There are enormous reserves of creative potential so that we may improve every area of our life. One good idea is all you need to start a fortune.

Continue personal development. Read books and magazines that enrich your mind and develop your skills. Listen to audiocassettes, attend seminars and workshops.

Be an unshakable optimist. Build these essentials for success: self-confidence, self-trust, and self-esteem. Develop positive mental attitudes by expecting to gain something from every situation and by always looking for the good in each one.

Dedicate yourself to serving others. Develop an obsession for customer service. Think of ideas that will serve people better in some area. Lose yourself in work that you feel will benefit others in some way.

Develop a reputation for speed and dependability. Develop a sense of urgency, a basis for action, and a drive to move quickly when opportunity or duty presents itself.

Be honest with yourself and with others. Successful businesses are built on trust with customers, suppliers, and others. Most business owners experience many ups and downs, but as long as they have the trust of people they can usually draw on the resources they need when they need them.

Concentrate on one thing at a time. Set priorities on all tasks. Do first things first and do one thing at a time. Don't diffuse your efforts by trying to do several things at once. Always focus on the valuable use of time.

Be decisive. Take time to think before you act. Be quick on your feet, willing to make mistakes, to admit error, and to change your mind. Remain fluid, flexible, and adaptable.

Back your plans and goals with persistence and determination. Make up your mind that you will never give up. Develop the courage to persist in the face of adversity and disappointment. Persistence is a true measure of your belief in yourself and your ability to succeed.

Discipline yourself. Develop the strength of will to force yourself to pay the price of success—doing what others don't like to do—going the extra mile and fighting the uphill battle yourself.

*   *   *

Becoming a Millionaire

Some years ago, when I was president at Edward Waters College in Florida, I attended a commencement speech given by my good friend, J. E. Davis, who was Chairman of the Board of the Winn-Dixie Stores. His nephew, Robert Davis, served as chairman of the Development Board at my college.

In approximately 20 minutes, Mr. Davis gave the best speech I have ever heard on the characteristics and attitudes it takes to become a millionaire. In essence, he said that it is a highly competitive world and becoming a millionaire won't be easy and that fear is a very essential element of success. His version of Murphy's law is—"Anything bad can happen and will happen." In his speech, Mr. Davis listed the personal traits one must develop to become a millionaire:

> I say to any person . . . that if he expects to make a success through government paternalism, he is doomed to disappointment. First, the person must decide definitely and

quickly what business he wishes to follow. Then forgetting obstacles and ailments he must apply his mind to learning every detail of that business, in and out, backward and forward. He must not let his love of golf, or tennis, or card playing or gambling, or even his wife, take his eyes from his objective. He must devote day and night to the task of finding out what makes his business tick or what is needed to make it grow.

At the top of the list is CHARACTER. Let's define character as something in your brain or heart that controls what you do when absolutely no one will ever know if you do wrong.

You must develop GOOD JUDGMENT. It has been said that good judgment comes from exercising poor judgment and not making the same mistake twice.

A most desirable characteristic is the ABILITY TO HANDLE PEOPLE—our relations with our associates and even our family.

FAIRNESS is probably the most important ingredient in human relations. You must learn to be fair to your associates and work at binding them together, moving toward established goals.

MORALE is one of the keynotes in any business enterprise. Do not be afraid to dish out liberal doses of encouragement.

Most important, you cannot be a millionaire unless you are a dedicated CAPITALIST, and learn to handle money. Remember, YOU CANNOT BE A MILLIONAIRE WITHOUT MAKING AND SAVING $10,000 FIRST. To become a capitalist is simple—just maintain the income over the outgo. Hire money when you can use it at a profit—never borrow money to live on. Cut your spending or up your earnings. If you can't do this, you will never be a millionaire. If you don't have a financial plan, make it right now.

Your biggest hurdle in business is to get all the factors together and organize them so you can pay the bills out of the receipts. I think I could run almost any business if somebody would pay the bills.

An important tool of success is keeping your education up to date by reading. There is no terminal degree in education—it goes on for your entire life.

You must be an INNOVATOR—to be on constant search for better ways to do things. To be an innovator, you must be AGGRESSIVE, TOUGH-MINDED AND PERSISTENT.

Time is the most precious thing in the world—you must have the ability to make use of it efficiently.

These are some old fashioned ideas in simple language that you need to adopt as policy:

Honesty is not only the best policy—it is the only one for success in life. Don't give your word carelessly, but if you do, keep it. Keep appointments, be dependable, be on time. A fair day's work for a day's pay and a fair pay for a day's work.

I've heard that the great inventor, Thomas A. Edison, said "Genius is 1% inspiration and 99% perspiration."

The most dangerous drug of our times is not a hard drug, but a drug called "SFN"—Something For Nothing. Don't get addicted to it, or you will never become a millionaire.

There is no such thing as "it can't be done"—problems are unsolved opportunities. Someone is going to solve great problems and be liberally rewarded.

The *"I will"* is worth more than *"IQ"* but together they are unbeatable. Real motivation to get results will make life interesting.

In the parlance of the grocery business, there are 57 rules for success—the first one is to do a good job. Don't worry about the other 56!

BABY BOOMER STRATEGY PLANNER

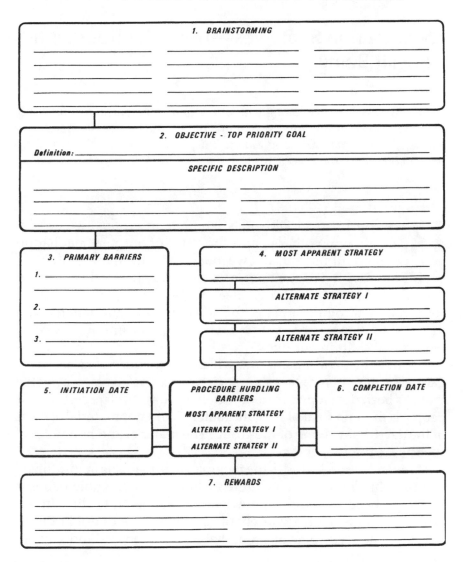

Chapter 14

Social Action Strategies—The Baby Boomer as a Social Being

Our success in getting along with others and communicating effectively with them depends upon the same principle used by successful salesmen, teachers, doctors, lawyers, and others. It depends upon our ability to help other people solve their problems.

Because we are social beings who live in groups, we are dependent upon other people for much of our personal happiness and fulfillment, and we must work effectively with other people in order to engage in careers and jobs effectively and competently. The foundations of civilization itself rest upon an ability to cooperate with other humans and to coordinate our actions with theirs. Thus, there is no way to overemphasize the importance of interpersonal skills in our lives.

The human environment into which we are born consists of organized groups of individuals (a society) and a particular way of life that has been developed by that society (a culture). The culture of a people is the sum total of both the material and nonmaterial aspects of the day-to-day living of the group. The material and nonmaterial aspects are interdependent.

Material culture includes the tangible man-made or man-utilized objects, while nonmaterial culture includes the intangible patterns of living—beliefs, attitudes, knowledge, customs, and habits. In any group of people, a great variety of common ways of doing things develop. These customs or group habits of action and thought are called folkways.

There are many factors involved if Baby Boomers are to survive and flourish in the social arena. It seems evident that three of the major problems that will be encountered will involve the family (usually a spouse and children), employment, and aging parents.

The nuclear family doesn't exist to the same degree that it used to. Less than 50 percent of families actually fit the description of a nuclear family with two parents as head of the household. There is a high divorce rate among Baby Boomers, and there are many causes for divorce. The three major causes are communication, finances, and sex. The most common cause is communication—or, more specifically, lack of communication. If communication is good, the other problems can usually be worked out. Therefore, in this chapter we will review some of the strategies to improve communication skills.

Another area of social stress involves employment and the changing job market. Many downsizings, mergers, restructuring, outsourcing, and other factors in recent years have made employment less secure than in the past. This trend is expected to continue well into the next century.

An increase in female employment and the growing success of many women in the workplace and in various professions have created a problem for some men who in the past were viewed as the chief breadwinner of the household. Now, many women earn more than their husbands and are able to adjust more readily to the computer/information age than their spouses. We will examine some of the strategies for survival in this area.

Since people are living longer, Baby Boomers will have to deal with the problem of caring for, or making arrangements to care for, aging parents. Strategies for survival and handling these problems will also be explored.

Changing Employment Outlook for Baby Boomers

There is a big psychological phenomenon happening in our society right now as many men feel they are rapidly losing ground in employment. According to the Bureau of Labor Statistics, women still earn less than men, although their wages have grown faster. From 1979 until 1994, the median full-time weekly salaries of women increased 123%. During the same period, men's wages increased only 85%.

The opportunities for women are much greater now than ever before. Not only are there more women in all the major professions, but there are many women entrepreneurs. During the past decade, women have formed far more new businesses than have men. This phenomenon has caused a number of men to feel sort of defeated and depressed. If the male Baby Boomers don't have a considerable amount of education and if they aren't growing or re-training themselves for the jobs of the future, they will have less opportunities for employment.

One of the reasons that women have been so successful during this information age is because of their good skills in interpersonal communication. If the Baby Boomer male is to be successful in the future, he will need to learn from the females in the area of communication.

Mid-Life and the Baby Boomer

The years between the ages of forty and fifty have been referred to as a period of crisis and dramatic change, some of which can be rather stressful. As you become aware that you are beginning to grow older, birthdays tend to be seen from a different perspective— a measure less of time lived than of time remaining. Sometimes the awareness of the shortness and fragility of life is highlighted by the serious illness or death of a close relative or friend who was near your own age or only a few years older.

Many Baby Boomers at this age will reach a plateau in their careers and a limit in their vocational potential. Some who may have been focused on climbing the career ladder may shift to other things in life that they have missed out on. Some may wonder if it's too late to begin a new career. Some who have concentrated on child rearing in the past will begin to worry about what to do when the children have left the nest.

Between the ages of forty and fifty, both men and women begin a serious re-examination of their lives and may decide to make significant changes regarding their careers or families. In the past, women, perhaps more than men, had a tendency to become depressed during middle age. Current research tends to suggest that contemporary women are more likely to experience middle age as liberating. Many women now have careers of their own and do not feel the middle-age crisis as much as their mothers and grandmothers did.

During this period of their lives, Baby Boomers can expect an improvement in their relationship with their own parents and with their adult children, especially if they live under separate roofs. However, these family ties can often be quite stressful if the Baby Boomer has to provide financial and emotional support for both their parents and their adult children.

Baby Boomers as Caregivers to Aging Parents

Because of the increasing longevity of the average American, many Baby Boomers are becoming concerned about the potential role and responsibility of providing care for their parents. The research literature indicates that actual caregiving to aging parents comes at a high psychological price. The overall stress that is expressed as feelings of anxiety and depression about caregiving by an adult child stems primarily from two sources.

First, Baby Boomers may have trouble coping with a decline in their parents' functioning especially when the decline involves cognitive abilities. Second, they are likely to feel anger, guilt, anxiety, and depression when they view the situation as confining or infringing on their time as a spouse, parent, or employee.

Anxiety can become a serious malady for those caring for parents with chronic conditions such as Alzheimer's disease, heart disease, diabetes, or other chronic illnesses that affect so many of the older generation. The stress levels are especially high for adult daughters who are expected by other family members to assume the role of primary caretaker for an aging or ill parent.

Several family-based and external strategies are available to address the needs of caregivers. The following are some of the strategies that have been shown to be effective:

- Open and honest communication with all family members
- Scheduled, uninterrupted time with one's spouse, children, and friends away from caregiving duties and responsibilities
- If possible, a specific schedule devoted exclusively to the care-recipient rather than an open-ended "be there at all times" situation
- An established source of social support outside the family

Although none of these strategies is perfect, adopting these and others tailored to the situation can lower the likelihood of conflicts.

Baby Boomers and the Future of the Family

Family life in America rests upon three institutions—dating, courtship, and marriage—that contribute much to the success or failure of that life. Marriage is regarded as essential by society to control the expression of the sex drive, assure the continuance of the group, and fix responsibility for the care of children.

Like marriage, the family is regulated, protected, and aided by the state. Economic security for the family is bolstered by income tax provisions and by property laws. Children are aided in education and protected from maltreatment and harmful working conditions.

Despite all this help, family disorganization is sufficiently widespread in the United States to cause concern. Some authorities hold a pessimistic view of the future of the family. An increase in the divorce rate is related to such conditions as:

- Lack of education about marriage and the family
- Weakening of family unity because of loss of certain family functions and because of the freedom among the members
- Smaller-sized or childless families, and
- Less social stigma on divorced persons

The impact of divorce upon children may be serious, because they must divide their loyalty between mother and father.

The research information on Baby Boomers shows that most of them are married or plan to marry eventually. However, the divorce rate of Baby Boomers has increased dramatically over the past thirty years. There are many reasons for the break-up of marriages, and research studies indicate that both sexes have quite similar complaints. For example, in one county in Wisconsin, everybody who filed for a divorce was asked the reason for the marriage failure. Of the top ten reasons for the divorce, 70 percent stated that it was a communication problem.

In his book, *Nonverbal Communications,* Dr. Jurgens Ruesch says that we communicate by means of some seven hundred thousand nonverbal signals. Now, when we consider the vocabulary of the average person, it is easy to understand why nonverbal communication has more effect than most of us realize. People, whether they know it or not, telegraph their intentions and feelings. Whatever occurs on the inside shows on the outside. We receive most of these nonverbal communications below the level of conscious thought. Our subconscious, computer-like minds evaluate them, and serve them up to us as "feelings."

The great French aviator and writer, Antoine de Saint Exupery, is reported to have said, "Marriage is not looking at each other, but looking in the same direction together." This is just as applicable to other aspects of life as it is to marriage.

Baby Boomers and Retirement

The older members of the Baby Boomer generation, which is made up of at least 76 million people, are already nearing retirement at a time when the institution of retirement itself is undergoing a transformation. As millions of Baby Boomers reach retirement age, major changes will occur in the way Americans retire.

A fifty-year trend toward early retirement bottomed out in 1985. Rather than retiring abruptly and at earlier and earlier ages as many in their parents' generation did, Boomers will stretch out their working lives, moving in and out of new and varied careers. "They're likely to view retirement as a process, not as a single event," says Boston College economist Joseph Quinn.

It is predicted that we will see a softening of the lines between being an active worker at age sixty-five and sudden, full retirement. Some Boomers will continue to work full-time, some will take part-time positions, some will spend their free time doing volunteer work, and a few Boomers will probably do all of these things.

A federally funded, landmark Health and Retirement Study based at the University of Michigan, shows that "a lot of people are retiring partially, or into 'bridge' jobs," says director Robert Willis.

People with good education who hold white-collar jobs and who are in good health—a description that applies more to Boomers than to preceding generations—are more inclined to continue working. However, not all experts believe that Boomers will want to continue working full-time until they drop. Cheryl Russell, editor of the *Boomer Report* says, "They're sick to death of the workplace, the frantic schedule. Most Boomers will embrace retirement. It's going to be like being a kid again and having your summers off." And, she adds, "It will be interesting to see what Boomers do with so much free time. The last time they had such free time [in their youth], they turned society upside down."

Helen Dennis of the University of Southern California's Andrus Gerontology Center says most people retire when they feel economically secure and qualify for benefits. "There's a good chance Boomers will retire when given the opportunity," she says. "The key is can they afford it?" Surveys show Boomers will work longer partly to finance their lifestyle expectations in retirement.

Developing Effective Communication Skills and Strategies

Our success in getting along with others and communicating effectively with them depends upon the same principle used by successful salesmen, teachers, doctors, lawyers, and others. It depends upon our ability to help other people solve their problems.

Carl Rogers, a noted psychologist, conducted a series of studies several years ago on how individuals communicate with each other in face-to-face situations. He found that the categories of evaluative, interpretative, supportive, probing, and understanding statements encompass 80 percent of all the messages sent between individuals. The other 20 percent of the statements are incidental and of no real importance.

From his observations of individuals in a variety of different settings, he found that the responses were used by individuals in the following frequency:

1. evaluative was most used
2. interpretative was next
3. supportive was the third most common response

4. probing the fourth, and
5. understanding the least

Finally, he found that if a person uses one category of response as much as 40 percent of the time, then other people see him as always responding that way.

The categories of response are in themselves neither good nor bad. It is the overuse or underuse of any of the categories or the failure to recognize when each type of response is appropriate that interferes with helping the sender and building a better friendship.

The major barrier to mutual understanding is the natural tendency to judge, evaluate, approve, or disapprove of the messages of the sender. Avoid giving evaluative responses in the early stages of a relationship or during a conversation about the sender's problems. The primary reaction to a value judgment is another value judgment (for example, "you say I'm wrong, but I think I'm right and you're wrong"), with each person looking at the issue only from his point of view. This tendency to make evaluations is heightened in situations where feelings and emotions are deeply involved, such as when you are discussing a personal problem.

The former head of a large corporation during his term as professor at Columbia University stated that the two most important areas of development in the future will be the collection of data for business and marketing and the study of the motivation of people. Studies conducted by major universities and business organizations indicate that less than 10 percent of job failures are due to inability to master the technical aspect of the job. If those studies are correct, this means that more than 90 percent of such failures are due to lack of understanding of life, of people, and oneself, and the lack of motivation to acquire and to apply this understanding—to narrow the gap that exists between habitual performance and potential performance.

To improve your communications skills, practice asking openedended questions that begin with the words Who, What, When, Where, Which, Why, How, and If.

Open-ended questions are thought-starters. They can't be answered with a simple "yes" or "no." Asking this type of question, whether of yourself or of another person, spurs the mind to action and produces the information essential to understanding any problem.

Using open-ended questions shows a person that you're interested in him or her. Intelligent, well thought-out questions get the other person "into the act." They are one of the best ways ever devised to get to know someone or to obtain information. Paradoxically, the person who's doing the talking admires the good listener and will begin to think of the good listener as a great conversationalist.

Chapter 15

The Importance of Relationships

"The quality of your relationships will largely determine how long you live and how well you live during that time."

—Brian Tracy

It is a well-known fact that men and women are gregarious animals who constantly seek the companionship, love, and friendship of other human beings, but did you know that the absence of close personal relationships and social support systems can actually shorten a person's life? A number of studies have been conducted over the years in this area. Here are some of the results:

- People with few close contacts, who live alone and who are socially isolated, are more likely to die prematurely compared to their peers who have happy and fulfilling relationships.
- Widows are more likely to die from every major cause of death than married women.
- Men who divorce and who don't remarry are more likely to die from such diseases as stroke, heart disease, and cancer than do married men. (One reason married men fare better may be because their wives play a role by helping them take better care of their health and by insisting that they get regular check-ups thus detecting some of the life-threatening diseases at an early stage.)
- Elderly men and women have been shown to live longer if they have a pet.
- People who find comfort in religion and who are actively involved in a church, synagogue, or mosque are more likely to live longer after surgery than patients who aren't spiritual.

If you take the time to analyze each of these statements, you will realize that the key in each example is connectedness—having a connection, a relationship, to an individual person, a group of persons, or simply to a pet.

If relationships are as vital to a person's well-being and to life itself as the previously stated facts would seem to indicate, then how can we begin to develop better relationships? Is getting along with other people an inborn trait or is it a skill, or a group of skills, that can be learned or taught? What are the basic personality and character traits needed in order to develop meaningful friendships?

- *A positive mood and an outgoing personality are important factors.* If you are an irascible curmudgeon who is suspicious of everyone and everything, you are not going to make very many friends who are going to care about you in your periods of personal peril and distress.
- *Trust is another key to success in building caring relationships and friendships.* Develop a reputation for being fair and square in everything you say and do.
- *Honesty goes hand in hand with trust.* Be consistent and dependable. Don't lie, prevaricate, or exaggerate to yourself or to your friends and acquaintances.
- *Respect your friends and colleagues and their opinions even when you strongly disagree with them.* They have a right to their opinions, and they have a right to express themselves without your getting angry or exasperated and calling them an idiot or some other derogatory name. Try to see their point of view.
- *Learn to communicate.* All too often when friends have a conversation, it turns out to be two monologues rather than a dialogue. One friend will talk for awhile about his or her problems or triumphs and all the while the other friend is not really listening but is thinking about all the things he or she wants to talk about as soon as the first person stops. Learn to listen with your total attention directed to the other person; forget about yourself for a little while.
- *Express your appreciation to your friends at every opportunity.* Let them know that you care about them and that you are appreciative of their friendship and of everything they do for you, large or small. Thank them in person and remember to acknowledge in

an appropriate way some of the important dates in their lives such as birthdays and anniversaries.

- *Be helpful and willing to step in and go the extra mile for your friends even when you aren't specifically asked to do so.* Sometimes being helpful in little ways is what means so much to the other person.
- *Don't gossip.* It's a known fact that the people who gossip with you today will gossip about you tomorrow.
- *Don't be jealous or critical.* If a friend or colleague comes into some good fortune, try to be genuinely happy for them and let them know that you share in their joy.

How to Develop a Social Support Network

It's a simple procedure, really—get involved, become more active, and join organizations with whose philosophy and purpose you agree. Volunteer your time and talents with such groups as Habitat for Humanity, the Council on Battered Women, or Mothers Against Drunk Drivers (MADD). These, and hundreds of similar organizations, probably already have branches in your community. If not, get together with a few of your friends and investigate starting a local branch.

Don't spread yourself too thin, however. Don't join groups just for the sake of listing a lot of organizations on your résumé. The best way to build a personal support system and network is to become active in a few groups so you can get to know the other members or volunteers on an individual basis.

The Family and the Home

For the most part, healthy individuals do not develop by accident. Research shows that they are usually raised in homes that exhibit certain factors, including the following:

- *Communication is open and direct.* Parents do not talk to each other through their children nor do they talk about their children in front of them as if they were not present.

- *The home atmosphere is characterized by a substantial degree of warmth.* The family members have a capacity to understand what others are feeling and to communicate empathetically. Interest in and caring for one another are expressed in touching as well as in words and tone. Expression of emotion is more often positive than negative.

- *Individuality and autonomy are encouraged.* There is a high tolerance and respect for a person's right to differ verbally and to be different from other family members in taste, values, or behavior so long as it is not destructive to the self or others.

- *Power is shared in a good marriage, which results in a more stable home environment.* Circumstances, rather than a rigid code, decide which marriage partner exerts the greatest influence or power in a given family situation. No one member should always be dominant or submissive regarding family issues or tasks. The children cannot learn to respect authority when power is expressed by either or both parents in a rigid, harsh, tyrannical, inconsistent, and unjust fashion. They will become confused and may build up resentments that are expressed destructively, now or later, towards themselves or others.

- *Household responsibilities are shared.* Even very young children can learn responsibility by being assigned certain chores or tasks that they have to perform on a timely basis.

- *The parents provide emotional sustenance and nurturing for their children.* In a family where one parent is rejecting and domineering and the other parent is absent, meek, submissive, or nonsupportive, there is much less opportunity for the children to be nurtured towards emotional and attitudinal health. In such families, the child's self-image will not be a good one. In healthy families, pain, hurt, sadness, tears, and disappointment are more openly and immediately shared.

- *The family develops a capacity for acceptance of loss.* There is preparation for and acceptance of the separation from the family as each child grows up and leaves home and for the eventual death of each family member over time.

- *The parents instill in their children a capacity for joy in living.* If a family is able to enjoy living and growing together despite economic circumstances and the problems of life, the individual members of the family can face the fact that life is not easy and can live with hope and optimism rather than hopelessness and despair. Such persons can enjoy what there is to enjoy and accept what needs to be accepted while using their energies to attempt to change that which needs to be changed.

- *Development of a sense of humor and of "playfulness" will be a lifelong benefit.* Those who have learned to have a sense of humor as they grow up are better equipped to carry that sense of humor and goodwill into later life.

EXERCISE 15.1—Rating Yourself as a Friend

1. How important are friends to you? (check one)
   Very important _____
   Somewhat important _____
   Not important _____
2. Are you a naturally gregarious person who usually makes the first overtures in striking up a budding friendship with someone you have just met?
   Yes _____   No _____
3. Do you have a support group of friends that you can depend on?
   Yes _____   No _____
4. Can these same friends depend on you?
   Yes _____   No _____
5. Do you distinguish between the different demands and qualities of friends and acquaintances and give them time and attention accordingly?
   Yes _____   No _____
6. Do you limit your friendships for fear that if you get too friendly with too many people they will make too many demands on you and take up too much of your time?
   Yes _____   No _____
7. Do you find time in your busy schedule for your best friends to tell you their problems, hopes, and dreams rather than constantly talking about yourself?
   Yes _____   No _____

Scoring: Add up your Yes answers to questions 2–7. If you have answered Yes to five or more of these questions, you obviously value friendship and you probably have a lot of good friends and a lot of satisfying relationships.

If you had more No answers than Yes, you need to work on your friendships and relationships.

BABY BOOMER STRATEGY PLANNER

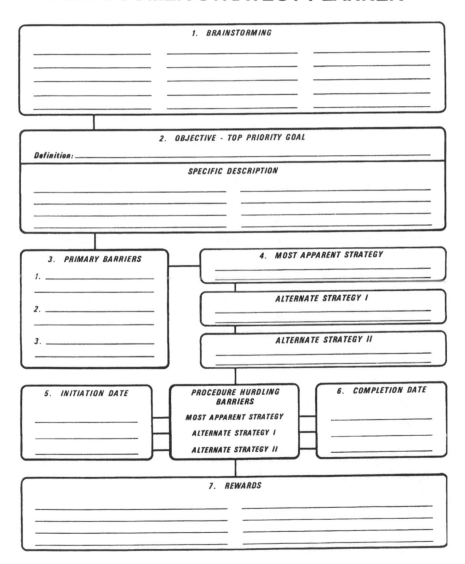

Chapter 16

Spiritual Action Strategies

"Man is more than mind and body, he is also spirit."
—*Earnest Holmes*[1]

There are three channels through which knowledge comes to us, namely science, philosophy, and religion. Science is an organized knowledge of natural laws and their applications to life. Philosophy, in simple terms, means the opinions we hold about the world, life, and reality. The term "religion" encompasses a vast panoply of beliefs about man's relation to the invisible universe. In other words, religion is man's idea of God or gods.

There are many philosophies and many religions, since in both instances they constitute opinions. Not so with science, however, for science is knowledge of the laws of nature. Once a principle is discovered and the laws governing it are ascertained, the scientist maintains absolute faith in that principle.

For most of history, religion and science have been divided into separate ideological camps. Many scientists have concluded that because the birth, structure, and functioning of the universe can be rationalized and explained by the laws of physics alone, there is no need to believe in the "myth" of a creator God or in the existence of a spiritual power or force in the universe.

More and more, however, theology and science are entering into a new relationship. A number of prominent scientists now are willing to concede that there does appear to be a design and purpose in the universe. Physicists have noted signs that the universe is custom-made for life and consciousness. If the constants of

---

[1]Earnest Holmes, *Good For You*, Science of Mind Publications, 1987.

nature—such as the strength of gravity, the charge of an electron, and the mass of a proton—were the tiniest bit different, then atoms would not hold together, stars would not shine, and life would not occur.

There's More Going on Than Our Senses Perceive

Our view of the world stems primarily from what we perceive through our five senses—what we can see, touch, taste, smell, or hear.

Unfortunately, our senses are limited; therefore, our view of the world is limited. This is not a problem unless we start believing that what we perceive is all there is to be perceived. Right now, there are hundreds of voices, pictures, and songs filling the air around us, but we are unable to see or hear any of them. The reason we don't know they're there is because our senses are unable to perceive these signals.

If we turn on our TVs, however, we could tune in these "waves of energy." The TV would translate what our senses cannot perceive into what they can. The fact that we can't see or hear these waves without a TV doesn't mean they're not there. They are; we are just not able to perceive them.

Thus it is with all sorts of natural and human-made phenomena. If we have the proper instruments, we can perceive them. If not, we are mostly unaware of their existence.

Dogs smell and hear better than most humans. Cats see better in the dark. Birds are more sensitive to movement. Even flies and small bugs seem to "know" when you're about to swat them.

The point is simple: *there's more to life than meets the eye.*

Understanding the Spiritual Laws

During the thousands of years that *Homo sapiens* have inhabited our planet Earth, many different names have been given to the Higher Power in the universe: Energy, Principle, Universal Intelligence, Universal Mind, Universal Being, Consciousness, Great One, Great Spirit, Jehovah, Yahweh, Allah, and God.

Just as there are many different names for "God," the concept of "spirituality" also takes on different meanings to different people. For some, it is a belief in God the Father and his son, the Christ. For others, it is simply a belief in a higher power or something greater than oneself that can be called upon for support or inspiration. Still other philosophies view spirituality as being in tune with nature or a state of internal peace developed from directing one's energy internally. Despite differences in doctrine and core beliefs, there is a commonality that unites most theologies. This is the peace and harmony with self and one's environment.

One of the most important concepts to understand is that there are irrefutable spiritual laws just as there are irrefutable physical laws. For example, the spiritual law of "you reap what you sow" can be understood by a simple, concrete example. A farmer has two seeds to plant—one is a seed of corn, which is something good, and the other is a seed of nightshade, which is a deadly poison. The farmer digs two holes and plants the corn in one and the nightshade in the other. Within a reasonable period of time, both seeds will sprout and grow because the earth does not discriminate between the good seed and the bad seed. It returns what was originally planted.

The mind operates in much the same manner. It returns to you what you have planted—negative thoughts or positive thoughts. You are the planter; therefore, in order to reap positive results, you must plant good and positive thoughts in your mind. This is a universal spiritual law that is psychologically sound because a person can attract certain positive or negative results.

How does one go about planting positive thoughts? In the Scriptures, Christ said that if you want something you must pray as if you already have it, and that which you are praying for will come to you. It may be difficult for you to believe that you have something when you know that you don't have it. Therefore, faith is very important. Affirming something is a statement of faith, and faith can be enhanced by affirmation and prayer.

In order to obtain what you are praying for, you should use the techniques of visualization and affirmation. In visualization, you must see and feel the object that is desired. In affirmation, you must say to yourself words that are personal, positive, and in the present tense. The subconscious mind does not recognize past tense or future tense. Therefore, you should say "I feel happy" rather than "I want to feel happy."

Your affirmations should be repeated as you are waking up or falling asleep when your mind is more suggestible. It has been proven by numerous studies of brainwave activity that when the brain is more relaxed, autosuggestions are more effective. If the brainwave pattern is recorded on a machine, the alpha state (which is the smooth brainwave pattern) is most effective in reaching the subconscious mind to plant the affirmations and positive thoughts.

The Power of Faith

Have you ever noticed that even the least religious of people will call upon their God in times of peril and distress. When there seems to be nothing humanly possible that can be done, people cling to the hope that a greater being—God—will intercede on their behalf. This hope is faith. By biblical definition, "faith is the assurance of things hoped for, the evidence of things unseen" (Heb. 11:1). Faith is intangible, it cannot be seen. Faith is not an intellectual concept, it is intuitive. It is a blind trust or belief in a power greater than self. Faith is integral to spirituality. Faith has consequences.

As recorded in the Bible during the ministry of Jesus, many of his healing events occurred because of the faith of the people, but even Jesus could not heal when the people did not believe or have faith. The one recorded time when Jesus was unable to perform miracles was when he visited his home village of Nazareth and his former neighbors scorned and rejected him.

Although we witness fewer modern-day "miracles," faith is still integral to having desires fulfilled. A key aspect of faith is patience; in fact, faith and patience go hand in hand. You must understand that God does not work in haste and you must remain faithful even if your desires aren't fulfilled within your timeline. It is akin to buying something on layaway. You are making payments on the object and although it does not yet sit in your home, you are confident that one day soon it will. You do not worry that you will not receive or own it—you know for certain that it belongs to you. You only await the time when you will pick it up.

Although success and failure are tied up in our thinking, faith and anxiety are contradictory. One cannot have faith and be anxious. People become anxious or fearful when they perceive a threat. If you are steadfast in your faith, there is no reason to feel threatened or to fear that you will not receive what your heart desires.

The Mystery and Power of Prayer

Whatever you ask for in prayer, believe that you have received it and it will be yours—Mark 11:24

People pray for many reasons—to give focus to their lives; for peace and prosperity; for forgiveness of sins real or imagined; for health, wealth, or success; for divine inspiration or guidance; or for communion with their creator. People pray because they believe that prayer not only changes things but also changes people.

How and where people pray is just as varied as their reasons for praying. Some prefer to pray alone, while others believe it is more powerful to pray as part of a small or large group. Some kneel, sit, stand in silence, or chant the formal rituals and prayers of their particular faith, while others who are as deeply spiritual believe the best place to pray is outside the confines of a church, synagogue, or mosque.

The question is often asked, is there a proper or "best" way to pray? Emory University theology professor Roberta Bondi says that people should not think they need rule books to address the Almighty. "There is no one right way to pray," she says. "If you are praying, you are already doing it right." Other research has indicated that positive prayer is most effective.

No matter how or where they do it, people still pray and they still believe in prayer. In a poll conducted by *Newsweek* magazine in March 1997, 54 percent of American adults reported that they pray daily, and 29 percent said they pray more than once a day. A whopping 87 percent said "they believe that God answers their prayers at least some of the time." In a poll taken by the *Atlanta Journal-Constitution* during late summer 1998, it was found that 90 percent of Southerners and 80 percent of people outside of the region believe that God answers prayer.

Intercessory Prayer

For the past several years scientists and others have been seeking proof that prayer really works. Some scientists claim that they have evidence that intercessory prayer—praying for another person or a group of people who may not even know that they are being prayed for—can help heal. Also, more and more medical doctors have become convinced that prayer can improve a person's health.

More than 250 studies have linked health to religion and prayer. In general, they tend to show that belief in God improves your health and may lead to a longer life. Keep in mind, however, that prayer is not a replacement for good medical treatment, but instead is a very effective addition to it. It makes good sense to use both.

In 1988, Dr. Randy Bird, a cardiologist at the University of California, San Francisco, published one of the first studies on intercessory prayer. He found that those who were prayed for had less need for respirators, required fewer diuretics, suffered less congestive heart failure, experienced less cardiopulmonary arrest, and became less ill with pneumonia.

One of the largest studies to date on intercessory prayer was conducted by Dr. Herbert Benson, a cardiologist at Harvard Medical School. He speculated that intercessory prayer works because of some unknown energy force that travels from one brain to another even over great distances.

A scientific investigation of prayer therapy was found to be effective in helping overcome problems by following some simple rules during prayer. An experiment in prayer was reported in the book, *Prayer Can Change Your Life* by Dr. William Parker and Elaine St. Johns. Forty-five troubled men and women were divided into three groups with fifteen subjects in each group. Group 1 used psychotherapy to solve their problems, Group 2 used random prayer for their problems, and Group 3 used prayer therapy for their problems.

The results showed that the group that used psychotherapy had a 65% improvement, the random prayer group showed no improvement, and the prayer group showed 72% improvement. An analysis was made to determine why the prayer therapy group succeeded and the random prayer group failed.

The random prayer group used a negative form of prayer. They repeated their unhappy symptoms, holding them in focus during their prayers. They confirmed their discomfort and hopelessness and accepted their suffering as punishment or a lesson. They began their prayer with an act of self-condemnation. It was found that negative prayer produced negative results.

On the other hand, the prayer therapy group made prayer positive. They prayed as if they were already in possession of that which they desired. Positive prayer produced positive results. The prayer therapy group recognized a God of Love within us, and prayer was a means of communication with God. For the people in this group, prayer was a regular activity, the last thing at night and the first thing in the morning. One of the keys to effective prayer according to this study is to use positive prayer.

The science of mind approach to successful living, as promulgated by Earnest Holmes, appears to be on the right path. For example, it is stated that our thoughts can help us in healing our bodies and in controlling the circumstances and situations around us. We can use the laws of nature consciously and decide what we want them to do for us, but we ourselves are not these laws. They are greater than we are, and we may have implicit confidence in them because we know they will never fail. We must recognize and accept that it is done unto us as we believe. According to this approach, when we pray we do something to our own mind to convert an old belief to a new belief. We convince our mind that the thing we desire is now here.

Earnest Holmes has divided Mind, or God, into three sections.

Conscious Mind—that which directs you.
Subjective Mind—that which obeys and creates.
Physical World—that which is created.

In summary, according to Holmes' philosophy:

Everything is mind and you are a part of it.
Mind responds and produces according to your believing thought.
You have the right and power to think what you want to think.
You control your own good and may transform your life into experiences of happiness, health and prosperity.
Mind responds to mind. It is done unto you as you believe. Therefore our bodily conditions are governed by our thought processes. This idea has been corroborated by psychosomatic medicine.

A good example of the success of prayer is the twelve-step program of Alcoholics Anonymous. The basic elements of their program involve surrender, relaxation, cleansing, and faith.

The following is an example of a prayer for physical health by Earnest Holmes.[1]

> I realize there is a Divine Presence at the center of my being. I let this recognition flow through my entire consciousness and flow down into the very depths of my being. Every thought and condition contrary to the Divine Perfection is eliminated. I rejoice in this realization.
>
> I now affirm that my body is a body of right ideas. It is now the Body of God. Its every action and function is harmonious. Whatever does not belong is eliminated. What needs to be renewed is renewed. All the energy, action, power, and vitality there is in the universe is flowing through this Divine creation now.
>
> I am now made vigorous and whole. I am strong and well. Every breath I draw is a breath of perfection, vitalizing, up-building, and renewing every cell of my body. I am healed and made whole in the likeness of Spirit. I have complete faith and acceptance that all the statements I have made are now fulfilled as I have believed.
>
> My word of acceptance does actually establish in my body the action and harmony which already exist. There is One Life—perfect, harmonious, whole, complete. That Life is my life now—not tomorrow, but today.

---

[1]Earnest Holmes, *Good For You*, Science of Mind Publications, 1987.

Chapter 17

Growing in Spirituality—Becoming a New Person

"It is possible to be the person you want to be and to accomplish whatever you want to accomplish. You must first make a conscious choice to begin a new life."

Scriptures tell us that as man grows closer to God, he is made into a new being. This does not mean that he miraculously does everything right—it means that he desires to make the necessary changes to continue growing and that he takes on actions and behaviors that allow him to free himself from his previous bondage.

Change is a difficult process. If you have been a slave to bad habits, actions, or behaviors, it is not easy to change these patterns. However, it is possible. It is possible to be the person you want to be and to accomplish whatever you want to accomplish. You must first make a conscious choice to begin a new life.

This spiritual birth is akin to physical birth in that it has various stages of development. Your acceptance of God's goodness and his will is your birth. Growing in oneness with God is similar to going through the stages of infancy, childhood, adolescence, and adulthood. It is a process facilitated by faith and by affirmations and denials. It is important not only to have new thoughts but new habits and actions as well. To have new thoughts without new actions is akin to putting new wine in old wineskins. The wineskins will break and all of the new wine will spew forth wasted. To make sure your new wine is in new wineskins, you must build yourself up with practice. You must embrace your newness. You must become a slave to good habits.

The Use of Denials and Affirmations

We have all heard the saying, "being in denial," which is used to describe someone who chooses not to believe something that seems apparent and real to everyone else. A denial is a statement used to cleanse your mind of wrong, negative, or somewhat limiting beliefs. A spiritual denial, for example, is a statement that repudiates old beliefs that limit us.

Many psychologists believe that denial can be both beneficial and detrimental. It is beneficial in that it is a defense that protects a person against harmful information. It is detrimental in that a person cannot cope with reality if he or she chooses to stay in denial.

Denials can be used to empower you physically. It is thought that the body controls the mind, but this relationship is bidirectional. Your thoughts can directly impact your health. Illness is an absence of health. You can give power to illness by embracing it or you can disempower illness by denying it. A denial to help you do this is— "Pain, sickness, poverty, and old age cannot master me."

No matter what you most fear in life, you can attack each fear with a denial. Tell yourself that "There is nothing to fear." Attack anger-provoking situations with a denial—"I won't let this bother me, nothing can steal my joy." If you are angry, stand still and deny the superiority of it over you, and the anger will leave you. If you are unforgiving and dwell on negative thoughts and sorrows of the past, denials will cleanse this negativity and unhappiness from your mind. Bad memories will become more distant as you use denials and affirmations.

Denials tend to erase, whereas affirmations build up. Affirmations are statements of faith that are utilized to bring something into existence. To affirm something is to believe that it exists even in the face of evidence that appears otherwise. You may not see how by simply affirming something to be true, you can bring it to pass. You don't bring it to pass—God fulfills the affirmation. The affirmation is a statement of faith. If you doubt your efficacy, give in too easy, or are anxious and fearful, affirmations will give you strength and courage. They will give you the power to change yourself. You will be able to affirm your desires and boldly claim, "It will happen." Pure faith, therefore, is the key to having your desires fulfilled.

Meditation

There are many forms of meditation, but what they all share in common is the practice of getting the most out of life. Many people erroneously assume that meditation is a religion. Transcendental meditation (TM), for example, is a scientific discovery that comes from India, but it is not simply a Hindu practice. In fact, TM does not involve any religious practices or beliefs. Religious leaders have indicated that the only thing TM has to do with religion is that it is the easiest technique discovered for making religion more meaningful by helping people live the way their religion teaches them to live through love and self-giving. People of all religions utilize the technique because it enhances clarity of mind, which can broaden the comprehension and appreciation of any religious practices.

TM is a technique that is simple, effortless, and natural. It not only enhances one's spirituality by making the mind clearer, it also gives the body deep rest and improves the coordination between mind and body. How well you perform at anything is dependent upon how rested you are. TM has been demonstrated to provide a unique kind of rest that surpasses the benefits produced by sleep. This rest removes deeply rooted stress that is not normalized during sleep.

Besides deep rest, there are additional benefits to TM. Psychologists estimate that under normal circumstances we utilize only 5 to 15 percent of our brain's capacity. By doing TM, some followers believe that you can come into contact with 85 to 95 percent of your brain's potential. TM cultivates the brain until it is available for your spontaneous use. Your mind becomes expanded and your awareness increases.

The correct practice of TM requires training with a qualified teacher. Usually four two-hour sessions will prepare you to practice TM. It is practiced twice daily during the morning and evening for 15 to 20 minutes each time. It can be practiced anywhere—at home, in your office, on the bus, in bed, on a park bench, and so on.

Although TM is the most researched meditation technique, there are other forms of meditation that can produce similar effects with respect to relieving stress and enhancing quality of life. One such form that is easily implemented is Mantra Meditation. This technique involves sitting quietly for 15 to 20 minutes and reciting a mantra (a word or a short phrase) over and over to yourself. Other meditation techniques involve use of visual imagery.

Practice meditation and see how it can enhance your life.

* * *

Whatever your own personal religious or spiritual philosophy may be, we hope you have read the previous sections with an open mind and that you will utilize the principles outlined to enhance your spirituality and quality of life. The exercises that follow will help you achieve this end.

STRATEGY 1—The Prayer Box

Some authorities have found the prayer box to be a successful strategy for strengthening their faith.

Create your own prayer box by writing down each of your deepest desires on a separate piece of paper. No matter how big or small the desire is, write it down. At the end of each statement, affirm your faith by claiming and writing, "And so it is."

Place all of these desires (or prayers) in a small box and keep it in a private place. Add to the box as your needs arise. Forget about the prayers in your box, no longer worry about them or give them undue attention. Instead, with faith, wait for them to be actualized.

At the end of each month, open your prayer box and see how many of your desires have been fulfilled. For those desires that have not been fulfilled, return them to the box and continue to be faithful and patient. Faith is a power that every person has, but few people use it correctly. The power of faith is illustrated by this poem:

> One ship drives east and another drives west
> with the self-same wind that blows
> Tis the set of the sails and not the gales
> which tells us the way to go.

This poem makes a good point. With a sailboat, you can go east or west—all with the same wind blowing in the same direction. It's all up to you.

STRATEGY 2—Becoming a New Person

To facilitate your desire to become a new person, write a statement of being. This is similar to a "mission statement" and will indicate who you are as well as your purpose and goals. You may write one statement and recite it daily or you can write a new statement each day, adding to the previous one. Use the following statements as a guide. Be sure to visualize and repeat your statements in the present tense as if you have already accomplished them.

Today I see myself as a new person beginning a new life.
I use meditation, prayer, and affirmations daily to enhance my spiritual development.
I cherish my body and practice moderation by not overindulging in harmful activities.
I am successful by practicing the art of faith and patience.
I am successful by forming good habits and planting the seed of accomplishment in every aspect of my life.
I am successful because God is in me and I am in God.

STRATEGY 3—Using Denials and Affirmations

Practice using denials and affirmations by reciting the following broad-based ones or create your own personal and more specific denials and affirmations. You can recite them as often as you need to, but particularly as you begin and end each day as a method of retraining your mind and enhancing your relationship with God. They will serve to deliver you out of distress when human help is not enough. Do not be anxious about receiving instant results or changing your beliefs overnight.

Denials

Pain, sickness, poverty, and old age cannot master me, for God manifests his perfect health within me.
There is nothing in the universe for me to fear, for greater is He that is within me than he that is in the world.

Affirmations

God knows my needs and will fulfill them.
I am a child of God and nothing can hurt me or make me sick or afraid.

STRATEGY 4—Practicing Mantra Meditation

Follow the following guidelines to practice Mantra Meditation:

1. Assume a comfortable position in a chair or lying down.
2. Close your eyes and relax as much as you can.
3. Focus on your breathing. Notice when you breathe in and out, paying attention to the sensation of air as it passes through your nose. Focus on the air coming in or out of your chest or your stomach. Try to breathe naturally, letting the air come through your nose and out of your mouth.
4. Each time you breathe out, repeat a mantra or word that represents the state you want to achieve such as "peace" or "love." Your mantra can also simply be a word or phrase with no particular meaning.
5. As you meditate, random thoughts will enter your stream of consciousness. As this happens, simply return your attention to your breathing and your mantra. As you continue meditating, you will experience fewer and fewer of these thoughts.
6. Practice this technique for 15 to 20 minutes in the morning and again in the evening.

STRATEGY 5—Developing an Enriched Spiritual Life

To develop greater faith and trust and a more balanced spiritual life, do the following:

• Pray and meditate daily
• Read and study the Scriptures consistently
• Attend religious services regularly
• Read inspirational books and magazines
• Participate in family or group Scripture reading, prayer, and discussion

- Think about and make a list of your own personal goals and objectives for achieving an enriched spiritual life. For example:
- Do you want to develop a deeper understanding of spiritual things or formulate a spiritual philosophy?
- Are you satisfied with the life that you now lead?
- Do you want to expand your grasp of the meaning and purpose of life?
- Do you want to be a tower of strength and encouragement to others?

Whatever it is you desire to achieve in this area, write your desires down, ponder them, and pray about them.

STRATEGY 6—Communicate with God by the Psychological and Spiritual Method

There are many rituals that various religious denominations have prescribed for their followers to communicate with God. A very simple effective method of communicating with the Creator has been summarized here based on ideas from many sources in the fields of psychology and religion. The great spiritual philosophers of every age have seen, sensed, and taught the same truth. They have told us of the wonderful relationship that exists between God and man and of the close union that cannot be broken. Some of the great teachers have consciously walked and talked with God just as we talk to each other. They revealed that it is possible for a person to talk with the Spirit because the Spirit is within all who believe in its presence. The whole philosophy of Jesus can be summed up in this simple statement: "It is done unto you as you believe."

1. In order to communicate with the Creator, it is an excellent idea to form the habit of getting up early in the morning for a period of time to meditate, plan, organize, and reinforce your faith every day. Sit in a comfortable chair and use the technique of relaxing your body as described in the chapter on stress relaxation. Once the body is relaxed, you may read or recite an inspiration mediation or a self-help meditation from the Bible or other sources.

2. During this faith period, you should imagine that the Creator is sitting in a chair in the room with you. Imagine that he/she is the very best and most loyal friend that you ever had; that he/she is the most intelligent person you know and who has all of the answers. Do not overcomplicate prayer. Think of it as a normal conversation between God and you. Simply talk to God through your thoughts in plain everyday English as a child speaks to his father. Do not feel that you must fill your prayer with stilted pious words.

3. There is no reason for you to carry the burden of your mistakes around with you all your life. If you can recall any mistakes, hostility, resentment, or hatred toward any human being, ask the Creator to lift this burden from you. Ask for forgiveness and have faith that you are forgiven. If you hold personal grudges or ill will, you can build a blockage that prevents spiritual power from getting through effectively. There is a divine power that responds to us despite our mistakes.

4. Give thanks for all the good things that happened to you the previous day. If some things are not as you would like them, thank God in advance for the good that is now working for you and that you believe will still come into being.

5. Express your concern for others such as those you love, the sick, those in need, and those you resent. God will always respond to you when you talk to him the right way. When you turn your thoughts to God, you are already communicating with him. Go inside yourself and you will meet God.

6. Turn your thoughts to your own needs, both personal problems and opportunities. Through your thoughts, request guidance and direction. The prayer for direction is vital to effective living and is one of the greatest sources of wisdom. Through prayer, you may receive guidance in all the problems and enterprises of life. Prayer should be direct and specific and should be accompanied by a positive receptivity. Jesus points out that God will answer when you pray correctly. When you pray, you are to believe that he has already given it to you, as stated in the Bible. "Ask and you shall receive. Seek and you will find. Knock and the door will be opened. For everyone who asks, receives. Anyone who seeks, finds." (Matthew 7:7-8). It is up to you to knock.

7. After you have completed the meditation and your prayers, you must now take action. Prayer is not something that we do to the Creator but to ourselves. Prayer does not bring about change unless we change our state of mind. "Faith is the substance of things hoped for; the evidence of things not seen." Faith is a faculty of the religious attitude, but always the man who has faith in his own ability accomplishes far more than one who has no self-confidence in himself. If we are wise, we must cultivate these realities. It is not just the words, but we must create the feeling through a multi-sensory procedure. As indicated in the mental strategies chapter of this book, you must begin to program your subconscious mind by continuously repeating all the sensory information you feed into it. Visualize and see yourself as already having whatever it is that you want to be, do, or have in your life experience. Verbalize—the subconscious accepts the words we use to program it. Therefore, use positive statements or affirmations to enhance your faith. As stated in the chapter on developing a success psychology, repeat your affirmation several times a day until your subconscious mind accepts them as reality. The subconscious responds even faster if you can involve your feelings and emotions. Try and use all of sensory modalities such as visual, verbal, touch, taste, and emotions to impress your subconscious. "According to your faith, so be it unto you."(Matthew 9:29)

What spiritual goals do I want to accomplish?

1.

2.

3.

4.

5.

What steps must I take to reach these goals?

1.

2.

3.

4.

5.

What are my target dates for reaching my most important spiritual goals?

1.

2.

3.

4.

5.

The Secret of Success and Happiness

There is an ancient legend about a time in the history of mankind when society so abused Wisdom that the Wisemen decided to take the secret of happiness and success away from man and hide it where he would never again find it. The big question was—where should they hide it.

A council was called by the Chief of the Wisemen to discuss this question. The lesser of the Wisemen said, "We will bury the secret of happiness and success deep in the earth."

But the Chief of the Wisemen said, "No, that will never do, for man will dig deep down into the earth and find it."

Then they said, "Well, we will sink the secret of happiness and success into the dark depths of the deepest ocean."

But again the Chief Wiseman replied, "No, not there, for man will learn to dive into the deep dark depths of the ocean and will find it."

Then one of the lesser Wisemen said, "We will take it to the top of the highest mountain and hide it there." But again, the Chief Wiseman replied, "No, for man will eventually climb even the highest of mountains, and find it, and again take it up for himself."

Then the lesser of the Wisemen decided to give up and concluded, "We do not know where it can be hidden. It seems that there is no place on the earth or in the sea that man will not eventually discover."

Then the Chief Wiseman said, "Here is what we will do with the secret of happiness and success. We will hide it deep inside of man himself, for he will never think to look for it there."

To this day, according to the legend, man has been running to and fro over the earth—digging, diving, and climbing, searching for something that he already possesses within himself. (Bland, 1978)

BABY BOOMER STRATEGY PLANNER

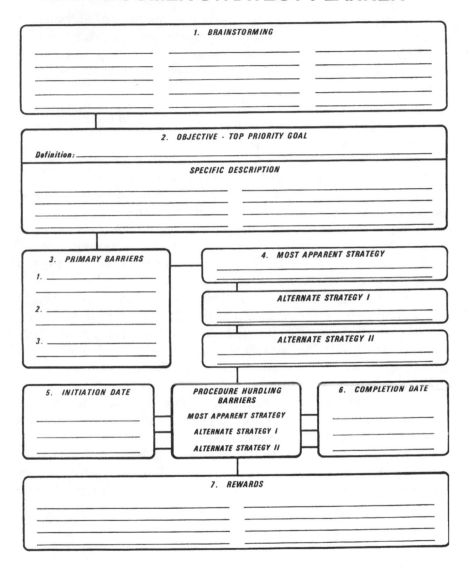

1. BRAINSTORMING

2. OBJECTIVE - TOP PRIORITY GOAL

Definition:

SPECIFIC DESCRIPTION

3. PRIMARY BARRIERS

1.
2.
3.

4. MOST APPARENT STRATEGY

ALTERNATE STRATEGY I

ALTERNATE STRATEGY II

5. INITIATION DATE

PROCEDURE HURDLING BARRIERS

MOST APPARENT STRATEGY

ALTERNATE STRATEGY I

ALTERNATE STRATEGY II

6. COMPLETION DATE

7. REWARDS

Chapter 18

Ethnic Minority Strategies

"He who starts behind in the great race of life must forever remain behind or run faster than the man in front."

—Benjamin E. Mays

"Summary of the World"

If the entire population of the Earth were shrunk into a village of 100 persons with all human ratios the same, there would be 57 Asians, 21 Europeans, 14 people from the Western Hemisphere (including North and South America), and 8 from Africa; 51 would be female and 49 male; 70 would be nonwhite and 30 white; 66 would be non-Christian and 33 Christian (no information about one person); 80 would live in substandard housing; 70 would be unable to read; 50 would suffer from malnutrition; one would be near death and one would be ready to give birth; only one would have a college education; and half of all the wealth would be controlled by six people, all of them U.S. citizens. (Landers, 1998)

OVERVIEW

Minorities are behind in the race of life and must run faster to catch up. The great scholar, W. E. B. DuBois, predicted that the problem of the twentieth century would be "the problem of the color line." Not only was his prediction correct, but regrettably it appears that the problem of race will remain with us well into the twenty-first century.

Let's take a look at some of the findings on African-American males from a report of the twenty-first Century Commission. Although this report was written in 1991, the findings are essentially the same today:

- African-American males have the lowest life expectancy of any group in the United States.
- Their unemployment is more than twice that of white males; even African-American men with college degrees are three times more likely to be unemployed than their white counterparts.
- About one in four African-Americans receive longer prison sentences than whites who have committed the same crimes.
- While suicide among whites increases with age, it is a peculiarly youthful phenomenon among African-Americans. It is the third leading cause of death of young African-American males; since 1960, the suicide rates have nearly tripled for African-American males and doubled for African-American females.
- Many African-American males die prematurely from twelve major, preventable diseases.

In addition to the dire plight of the African-American male, enumerated in the previous list, two additional statistical facts about African-Americans in general jump out at us:

- Nearly one-third of all African-American families in America live below the poverty line.
- Half of all African-American children are born into poverty and will spend all their youth growing up in poor families.

As we read these grim and shocking statistics, some 133 years since the abolition of slavery and 34 years since the passage of the Civil Rights Act, we must ask ourselves the question, why? Why are so many African-Americans still at the low end of the totem pole in terms of economic power, political clout, and social influence?

African-Americans are no different from any other human beings in that they are a product of both hereditary and environmental influences. At the same time, it must be acknowledged that many of the problems faced by African-Americans are precipitated by complex physical and social factors that produce a mutually reinforcing cycle.

First of all, as a society and as individuals, we have to confront the problems of racism. Racism is nothing less than a virulent cancer in American society. In this country, color or pigmentation has been a badge of inferiority for African-Americans for over 300 years, and color alone remains the basis for an oppressive and discriminatory social and political policy. All other things being equal, if you are defined as African-American, even if your actual skin color is barely black, your condition and your potential are significantly different from the condition and potential of a white immigrant or native.

Although racism has always existed in one form or another since the beginning of humanity, racism must be viewed as more than another nuisance. It is a barrier that has to be overcome. Laws and certain societal agencies and norms provide for institutional relief, but racism exists in the hearts, minds, and souls of people. It is based on few rational experiences and many irrational assumptions.

Partly because of racism and partly because of lack of education and the requisite skills, all too often African-Americans are still the last hired and the first fired from most jobs. It used to be that Americans with less formal education could depend on well-paying, union-protected, blue-collar jobs or the military to offer the potential for living a fairly decent life. As the economy of America has shifted to a service and technical base, the need for blue-collar labor is declining more and more each year. Skilled and inexpensive labor can now be obtained in other countries, and American businesses are realigning their production capabilities to take advantage of these lower labor costs. As a consequence, far too many African-Americans are stuck in menial jobs at minimum wages.

In American society today, the economic factor determines the neighborhood you live in, your friends, the schools your children will attend, and the types of nutrition and healthcare you are able to provide for your family.

The economic factor also impacts on many other variables because in our society a job, to a large extent, determines a person's social status. When you meet someone for the first time, it is inevitable that one of the first questions they will ask is, "What do you do for a living?" Depending on your answer (and who is doing the asking), you will be immediately pigeonholed into a certain classification, a sort of "hierarchy of personal worthiness" that has little to do with your actual selfhood or character.

Minority Baby Boomers and the Future

What about the future? Are conditions for the average African-American going to get better, remain the same, or deteriorate? What does all of this mean to the minority Baby Boomer in terms of income and quality of life?

For many African-American Baby Boomers, the outlook remains bleak. The Associated Press has reported that in a scientific sampling of 1,200 African-Americans, the majority thought that their conditions were worsening and that the American dream had become impossible to achieve. Along the same lines, a national study of African-American journalists reported "pessimistic" to "very pessimistic" views on the lack of improvement or an actual deterioration in nine of twelve institutional categories. One city editor stated, "I'm worried that the improvements in technology will allow us to minimize our interaction with people of various colors, creeds, and cultures. As a result, there will be more racial intolerance as people become more isolated and too self-absorbed to work for a greater, common good in society."

Another editor located in Seattle expressed his concern that racial divisions will deepen as illustrated in the aftermath of the O. J. Simpson verdict, and that "it will become tougher for people to afford health care, particularly as the Baby Boomer gets older."

Do these attitudes and opinions reflect reality? What are the positive changes that have occurred in recent years among African-Americans—and what does the future hold for our children and grandchildren?

First and foremost, one element that will play a significant role in the manner in which America deals with its racism is the fact that African-Americans will remain the largest and most dominant minority group in America for only a few more years. It has been projected that before the year 2050, "minorities" will comprise over 50 percent of the total population of the United States, and that Hispanics will be the dominant minority group, surpassing African-Americans as early as 2005.

Undoubtedly, the problems of African-Americans could be further compounded by the increased political and economic strength of Asians and Hispanics. The inevitable gains realized by Asians and Hispanics will have a profound economic effect on the political, social, and economic dynamics of American culture.

Another indication of the changing role in society of African-Americans is the tremendous gain in political clout of African-Americans during recent decades. In 1994, Manning Marable, history professor and director of the Institute of Research in African-American Studies at Columbia University reported that "Since 1964, the number of African-American elected officials has increased dramatically, from barely 200 to about 8,000 today. In that time, the number of African-American mayors has increased from zero to nearly 400."

Although far too many African-Americans fall into the "last hired, first fired" category mentioned previously, there is a large and growing African-American professional and middle class whose members have well-paying jobs, who live in large, beautiful homes, who travel frequently, and who have the time and money to indulge in the "finer things of life."

In this country, money is power, and African-Americans are now beginning to wield at least some small measure of financial power. *Black Enterprise* magazine has reported that African-American households have enormous amounts of disposable income, making them an attractive business market. The size of the African-American consumer market has in fact soared, from approximately $30 billion a year in spending nationally in 1964 to $270 billion in 1993. The purchasing power of African-Americans consumers has continued to skyrocket during this decade, thanks to a strong economy, a more open job market, and dramatic educational gains among African-Americans. African-American buying power—defined as total personal income after taxes—will surpass $500 billion in 1998, according to a University of Georgia study.

Economic power allows the ability to effect change and define reality. Unfortunately, however, reinvestment rates of African-Americans within their own communities, as well as general savings and personal investment rates, have been among the lowest in American households. Without this reinvestment for self-sufficiency in the future, it will be difficult for African-American households to maximize the fiscal and political strengths as successfully as other minority groups, such as Korean and Jewish Americans, have been able to do.

* * *

The focus of this chapter thus far has been a summation of the changing dynamics of American and international culture as it relates specifically to African-Americans. For the remainder of the chapter, we will emphasize those techniques and strategies that will play an important role in assisting all Americans, especially African-American Baby Boomers as they move toward the twenty-first century.

SURVIVAL STRATEGIES FOR AFRICAN-AMERICANS

- **Education—Education—Education.** To ensure economic security for yourself and your family, you have to invest in your most important asset—YOURSELF. As Americans live longer in general, the length of time that you will be working has also increased. In order to compete, you must continually upgrade your skills and knowledge because if you don't have the skills or education increasingly being demanded by American business and the military, you will not be able to capitalize on the opportunities that high-paying careers can offer. If you are a Baby Boomer without a college or graduate degree, don't despair. College or graduate school is definitely not for everyone. Some technical and trade schools offer the types of skills and training that are, and will continue to be, sought by employers. Many firms offer in-house training seminars, job enrichment programs, and cross training so you can perform in more than one position.

- **Commitment to Lifelong Learning.** "Education" must be viewed as a continuing process, not just a one-time event for young people. Our concepts of institutions of higher learning will be revolutionized by fast education methods through on-line education and distance learning. There is now a great profit potential for any business that can help others gain skills in their spare time. A commitment to lifelong learning and a strategy to improve oneself daily will be the only way to survive and advance in the twenty-first century.

- **Skill in More than One Job or Profession.** It is predicted that in less than twenty years, full-time or permanent jobs will become obsolete. Businesses will try to be more profitable by hiring temporary employees on a contract basis (i.e., to work on an assigned project until completed). Outsourcing will become the main source of employment. To compete, you will need to become proficient at a number of jobs so that when there is a decline in one area of employment, you can immediately switch over to another area.

- **Entrepreneurship—Starting Your Own Business.** As more and more people become disillusioned with the corporate world, entrepreneurship has become the current trend. It has been predicted that self-employment and home-based businesses will grow rapidly during the next decade. A recent article in a national publication stated that the majority of graduates of the nation's leading business schools want to start their own business and be their own boss. Furthermore, a large number of Baby Boomers, worried that the income they will receive after retirement from Social Security and their small pension will be not be enough to make ends meet, are planning to start their own businesses.

    There are many advantages to having your own business. For example, you can start a business at any age and can continue working in it until you decide when to quit, and you have the option of working out of your home to cut down on overhead and other expenses.

    If this is the route you hope to go someday, the important thing is, start planning for it now. Don't wait until you are a few months or a few weeks away from retirement to start thinking about what kind of business you would like to begin. There are literally hundreds of businesses that you can start on your own without having to go the franchise route, although that may be the best way for some people. Read magazines and books on entrepreneurship to give you ideas and steer you in the right direction.

    Dream big, but don't make the mistake of anticipating fame and riches from part-time self-employment. Be practical and realistic as you consider and discard various ideas and possibilities.

- **Computer Literacy.** To be competitive in the next century, you must become computer literate and find creative ways to make money by electronic communication. Millions of formerly skilled workers are being pushed out of the labor market and will be forced to take lower-paying positions because they do not have computer skills. One author has predicted that if you are not on-line now, you may be in the breadline tomorrow.

- **Networking.** Develop a network based on the old adage that "no man is an island." Networking is a tried and proven business strategy. Friends, family, neighbors, and co-workers can be excellent sources of support, information, contacts, ideas, and insider insights.

- **Political Involvement.** Minorities are not using their voting strength effectively. Minority Baby Boomers should use their economic and political power to help their cause. For example, if you don't vote, you don't count. Political candidates who are not committed to supporting programs that will help the minority community should not receive your votes or dollars. You need to support those candidates who are supporting childcare, education, housing, jobs for inner-city youth, and programs for the elderly.

- **Community Involvement.** No matter where you may be in your own life stage, you always have something to give. Someone, somewhere—a child, a teenager, a disabled person, a homeless person, an elderly person, a neighbor—can always benefit from knowing you and personally benefiting from your trials and challenges, your successes and failures, and the important lessons you have learned in your life. In many instances, they may seek nothing more from you than your abiding friendship as they attempt to deal with their own personal trials and tribulations.

  There are surely many programs in your own community or neighborhood sponsored by schools, churches, or civic organizations that would welcome your participation, even if it is for only a few hours a week or month.

- **A Secure Power Base.** This is just a fancy way of saying that you need some type of foundation to build upon and to realize your dreams. It is very difficult to progress and focus on the future if your personal life is in turmoil and disarray. This is the point where you need to assess and reassess your life to decide where you want to go and to eliminate and minimize those elements that are a distraction or barrier to your moving forward.

  This may require getting your financial house in order. It is very difficult to accomplish anything if you have to spend most of your leisure time worrying about paying your bills or if you have creditors and collectors harassing you. Nonprofit credit-counseling organizations can be a great first step to living within a manageable budget and enjoying the peace of mind that comes with fiscal responsibility.

Sometimes our personal lives are in disarray, because of a negative relationship or negative influences from friends, family members or co-workers. Managing personal and intimate relationships is very difficult, and actions you take to regain stability in these relationships is a reflection of your conviction and commitment. Once you get the basic elements of your life in an orderly and manageable state, you are free to move on to bigger and better things.

- **Proactive, Not Reactive Approach.** In the dynamic and competitive marketplace of America today, taking a complacent role leads only to stagnation or failure. Do not let others control you and your destiny. Take actions to advance your perspective and best interests. Take responsibility if you make mistakes. Learn from your mistakes and move forward.

- **Tolerance.** As a minority, particularly as an African-American, be assured that no matter what you do or how much you achieve, there is going to be somebody who just won't like you or respect you. DON'T TAKE IT PERSONALLY. It is their loss, not yours. As we discussed earlier in this chapter, the evil of racism exists, but you must not allow it to control your life and destiny or prevent you from achieving success.

  At the same time, don't fall into the invidious trap of blaming your own personal failures on the racism of other persons, groups, or organizations. In some instances, what you consider racism may be nothing more sinister than indifference or ambivalence to you or to your cause. Perhaps the person or group you consider racist doesn't even know you or have any particular motivation to know you. Even though they don't hate you, they just don't care. If you don't have anything they want, you are just immaterial and irrelevant.

- **A Positive Attitude.** No matter what type of situation you encounter, it is important for you to maintain a positive mental attitude. If the situation you are in is not a positive one, keep looking to see if you can find something positive about it. Live your life every day with the expectation that something good is going to happen to you.

  If you want to take this one step further, why not take a monthly calendar and jot down at the end of each day at least one good thing that happened to you during that particular day—perhaps you were told that you got a promotion or a salary increase at work, perhaps a friend you hadn't heard from in a long time called to say hello, perhaps a stranger made some unexpected gesture of kindness toward you.

The list of possibilities of "good things" could go on and on, and you may have a hard time choosing only one to write down each day. At the end of the month, go back over each item on your list and reflect for a few minutes on each of them. We are certain that after only one month of keeping track of the good things that have happened to you, you will feel more positive and optimistic—and more appreciative of the riches that come your way each and every day.

*   *   *

I want to end this chapter by telling you the story of little twin brothers, one a pessimist and the other an optimist.

> The little pessimist was always complaining and was very negative, while the little optimist viewed everything through rose-colored glasses. It was Christmas and their father decided to truly test their attitudes. He placed every kind of beautiful toy imaginable under the Christmas tree for the pessimist—a new bike, a basketball, a rifle, and dozens of things that would make a little boy happy. On the other side of the tree, he placed a pile of horse manure as the only present for the optimist.
>
> Early Christmas morning the father hid behind a sofa to watch the twins open their gifts. The pessimist entered the room first and saw all of the beautiful toys with his name on them. He began to complain, "If I take my new bike outside to ride and have a wreck, I might hurt myself and Dad sure would be mad. Oh, there is a basketball. I know that the first time I play with it I am sure to puncture it. Hey, there's a rifle, but I'd better not play with it because, as sure as the world, I'll break a neighbor's window . . . " and he went on and on, deep in negativism. Christmas morning to him was a disaster!

Then the little optimist came into the room. When he saw the pile of horse manure with his name on it, he enthusiastically began to run throughout the house, looking in all of the rooms, in the garage and in the backyard. When his father caught him by the arm and asked, "Son, what are you looking for?" the optimist replied, "Dad, with all that horse manure that I found under the tree, I just know there's gotta be a pony around here someplace!" (Bland, 1978)

BABY BOOMER STRATEGY PLANNER

1. BRAINSTORMING

2. OBJECTIVE - TOP PRIORITY GOAL

Definition:

SPECIFIC DESCRIPTION

3. PRIMARY BARRIERS

1.

2.

3.

4. MOST APPARENT STRATEGY

ALTERNATE STRATEGY I

ALTERNATE STRATEGY II

5. INITIATION DATE

PROCEDURE HURDLING BARRIERS

MOST APPARENT STRATEGY

ALTERNATE STRATEGY I

ALTERNATE STRATEGY II

6. COMPLETION DATE

7. REWARDS

Bibliography of Suggested Reading

Allen, Charles L. *God's Psychiatry.* Old Tappan, N.J.: Fleming H. Revell, 1953.

Allen, James. *As a Man Thinketh.* Old Tappan, N.J.: Fleming H. Revell, n.d.

Berger, K. S. *The Developing Person Through the Life Span.* New York: Worth Publishing, 1988.

Bland, Glenn. *Success.* Tyndale House, 1978.

Bloodworth, Venice. *Key to Yourself.* Los Angeles: Scrivener & Co., 1975.

Brande, Dorothea. *Wake Up and Live.* New York: Cornerstone, 1974.

Bristol, Claude M. *The Magic of Believing.* New York: Cornerstone, 1967.

Carnegie, Dale. *How to Win Friends and Influence People.* New York: Simon & Schuster, 1936.

Clason, George S. *The Richest Man in Babylon.* New York: Hawthorn, 1955.

Coon, Dennis. *Essentials of Psychology.* St. Paul, Minn.: West Publishing Co., 1985.

Corwell, Russell H. *Acres of Diamonds.* New York: Harper & Row, 1915.

Danko, W. D. & Stanley, T. J. *The Millionaire Next Door.* New York: Simon & Schuster, 1996.

DeVos, Richard M. *Believe!* Old Tappan, N.J.: Fleming H. Revell, 1975.

Fromm, Eric. *The Art of Loving.* New York: Harper & Row, 1962.

Hill, Napoleon. *Grow Rich with Peace of Mind.* New York: Hawthorn, 1967.

Hill, Napoleon. *Think and Grow Rich.* Greenwich, Conn.: Fawcett Publications, Inc., 1976.

Holmes, T. and Rahe, R., "The Social Readjustment Rating Scale," *Journal of Psychosomatic Research,* 1967.

Jones, Charlie. *Life is Tremendous.* Wheaton, Ill.: Tyndale House, 1968.

Maltz, Maxwell. *The Magic Power of Self Image Psychology.* Englewood Cliffs, N.J.: Prentice-Hall, 1964.

Maltz, Maxwell. *Psycho-Cyberbnetics.* New York: Pocket Books, 1970.

Mandino, Og. *The Greatest Salesman in the World.* New York: Bantam, 1974.

Nordhus, Inger and others. *Clinical Geropsychology.* Washington, D.C.: American Psychological Association, 1998.

Otis, George. *God, Money and You.* VanNuys, Calif.: Bible Voice, 1975.

Rosenfield, I., "When Impotence is Curable," *Parade Magazine*. New York: 1998.

Schuller, Robert H. *Self-Love: The dynamic Force of Success*. New York: Hawthorn, 1969.

Schuller, Robert H. *Move ahead with Possibility Thinking*. Old Tappan, N.J.: Fleming H. Revell, 1973.

Schwartz, David J. *The Magic of Thinking Big*. Englewood Cliffs, N.J.: Prentice-Hall, 1959.

Steere, Daniel C. *I Am-I Can*. Old Tappan, N.J.: Fleming H. Revell, 1973.

The Living Bible. Wheaton, Ill.: Tyndale House, 1971.

Tracy, Brian. *Insights into Achievement*. Chicago: Nightingale Co., 1996.

Tracy, Brian. *The Universal Laws and You*, Chicago: Nightingale Co., 1996.

Tracy, Brian. *Success Secrets of Self Made Millionares*, Chicago, Nightingale Co, 1997.

Whitaker, J. *Health and Healing*, Potaomac: Phillips, 1998.

Who is This Man Jesus? Wheaton, Ill.: Tyndale House, 1967.

Wright, Norman. *Improving Your Self-Image*. Irvine, Calif.: Harvest House, 1977.